10-Minute

Feng Shui

Room by Room

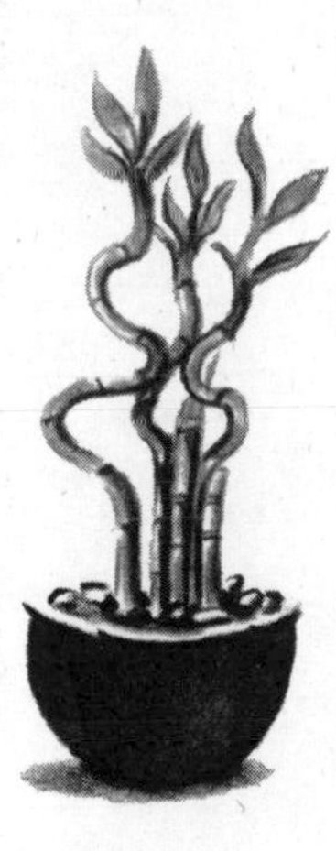

10-Minute Feng Shui Room by Room

Hundreds of Easy Tips and Techniques for Prosperity, Health, and Happiness

SKYE ALEXANDER

GLOUCESTER, MASSACHUSETTS

First published in the USA in 2006 by
Fair Winds Press, a member of
Quayside Publishing Group
33 Commercial Street
Gloucester, MA 01930

10 09 4 5
ISBN-13: 978-1-59233-187-1
ISBN-10: 1-59233-187-4

Library of Congress Cataloging-in-Publication Data
Alexander, Skye.
10-minute feng shui room by room : hundreds of easy tips and techniques for prosperity, health, and happiness / Skye Alexander.
p. cm.
Includes index.
ISBN 1-59233-187-4
1. Home economics. 2. Feng shui in interior decoration. I. Title.
TX147.A44 2006
133.3'337—dc22
2005024481

Cover Design by Laura Shaw Design
Illustration by Elizabeth Cornaro
Book design by Anne Gram

Printed and bound in USA

To the people who were there
when I needed you:
Lyndsey, Claire, Cally, June,
Ron and Lisa, Mamadou, Martin,
and my Al-Anon family.
Thank you.

Introduction

Feng Shui for Everyone

When I began studying feng shui more than two decades ago, most Westerners I mentioned it to had no idea what I was talking about. Many of them thought it was a Chinese entrée! Today, this term has become a household word, like pizza or déjà vu. A Google search turns up literally millions of references to feng shui. You can buy feng shui products at major discount department stores. Some of the most successful and powerful people and corporations in America now hire feng shui masters as routinely as electricians.

The main reason this ancient Chinese art of placement has found favor in contemporary Western society is that it works. Another reason is that feng shui "cures" are easy, quick, and inexpensive—many can be done in ten minutes or less, and they'll produce results in a matter of days. And feng shui's remedies are so versatile that there are usually dozens of ways to fix any given problem.

There's something almost magical about feng shui. That's because feng shui's power is rooted in your intention. The "cures" serve as tools to focus your mind. It will work even if you don't set your intention to change—but you'll get better and faster results if you combine the physical steps with sincerity, openness, and a willingness to change on a personal level.

In my earlier books, *10-Minute Feng Shui* and *10-Minute Clutter Control*, I introduced the basic tenets of feng shui. I showed you how to examine your home to determine which areas are causing problems in your life. In this book, I'll help you remedy difficulties and fine-tune your goals by applying feng shui's concepts in every room of your home. (But don't worry—you don't need the earlier books to use this one! I've included everything you need to know right here.)

Because my background is in interior design, I've chosen to include some solutions that combine feng shui's mystical properties with practical decorating tips. As many professionals in the design field have discovered, good interior design is good feng shui. That's why so many architects and interior decorators incorporate feng shui's tenets into their work, whether they realize it or not.

If you're interested in learning the fundamentals of feng shui, please read Part One before you start applying the cures in Part Two. If you already have a grounding in feng shui—or if you're the impatient type who wants to get started right away—turn to Part Two and choose the room-by-room cures that appeal to you. Don't limit yourself to the suggestions I've offered, however. As you become familiar with feng shui, feel free to design your own remedies. The best solutions are those you relate to strongly and personally. Be creative!

Skye Alexander

Skye Alexander

Table of Contents

Part One

Feng Shui and You

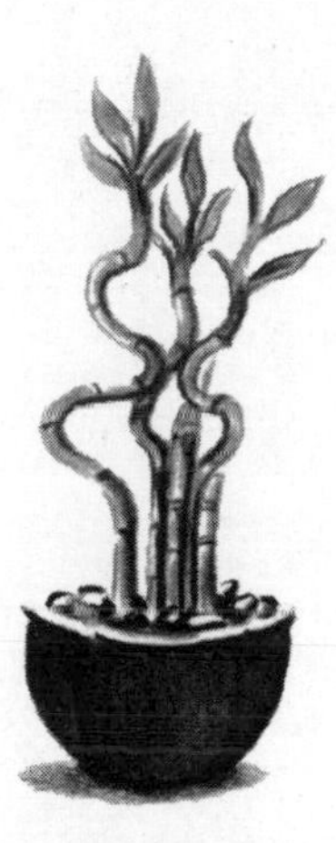

Chapter 1

How Feng Shui Can Help You

When Disney built a 310-acre, $3.5 billion theme park in Hong Kong, the entertainment giant consulted with a feng shui master to make sure everything from the opening date to the positions of the park's doorways were correct. Designed to be "the most harmonious place on earth," Hong Kong Disneyland is even sited in a location that's considered fortunate, according to feng shui.

Feng shui principles were a consideration for internationally renowned architect I. M. Pei, too, when he designed the Bank of China's tower in Hong Kong. Real estate tycoon Donald Trump says he uses feng shui "because it makes me money."

In recent years, many celebrities, including Oprah Winfrey and Steven Spielberg, have discovered the benefits of feng shui. So have some of the world's largest corporations—Coca-Cola, Sony, Shell, and Proctor & Gamble among them—which use it to boost profits, reduce employee turnover, and increase harmony within their companies.

If some of the richest and most famous people on the planet are turning to this ancient philosophy to enhance their success, there must be something to it. Shouldn't you find out whether feng shui can help you, too?

What Is Feng Shui Anyway?

Feng shui (pronounced *fung shway*) has been practiced in the East for more than 2,000 years. Rooted in the Chinese spiritual tradition Taoism and the teachings of Confucius, it literally means "wind and water." The goal is to direct *qi* or *chi* (also written as ch'i)—the vital energy that the Chinese believe animates all life on earth—through your environment so that its movement resembles a gently flowing stream or a pleasant breeze.

That's a very simple explanation for a complex and multilayered system, which contains many schools of thought and a wide range of practices, both practical and mystical. But underlying all of feng shui is a single, fundamental objective: to create harmony and balance in our environments and, by extension, in our lives. Properly utilized, feng shui lets us attract what the Chinese call the Three Great Blessings: health, wealth, and happiness.

Also known as the art of placement, feng shui gives us a formula for designing, arranging, organizing, and maintaining our homes and workplaces so they nurture us. Few environments are inherently ideal, but virtually all can be improved. Feng shui practitioners accomplish this by applying a variety of physical and psychological "cures," which I'll discuss more fully in Chapter 3, Fix Your Home, Fix Your Life (page 49) and in Part Two, Feng Shui Room by Room (page 81). (In my earlier books, *10-Minute Feng Shui, 10-Minute Clutter Control,* and *10-Minute Clutter Control Room by Room,* I also offer hundreds of simple feng shui cures you can do yourself to improve every area of your life.)

You don't have to be a master in this ancient art to experience its effects. To begin, all you need to do is pay attention to your feelings when you enter a space you've never been in before. A building that has "good feng shui" will make you feel welcome, comfortable, safe, and at peace. One with "bad feng shui" will stir up all sorts of unpleasant feelings—uneasiness, agitation, lethargy, apprehension, and/or discomfort.

As you learn more about feng shui, you'll start to notice even subtle disturbances in the homes, offices, and retail environments you frequent. You'll also start to see how to rectify those problems. "Once you begin to apply feng shui principles, you'll be able to flow smoothly with the river of life, rather than having to swim against the current," says New York feng shui consultant Benjamin Huntington.

Why Feng Shui Works

If you've ever studied the psychology of dreams, you know that the house is a symbol for your life. It's no surprise, then, that your physical home speaks volumes about you: It serves as a mirror that reflects images of the many facets of your daily existence. A feng shui master can look at your home and immediately see which parts of your life are operating smoothly and which parts are causing you problems.

The Chinese believe that all life is interconnected—our environments influence us, and we influence our environments. It's easy to understand how our environments affect us. We've all experienced the sense of serenity that comes from walking in a peaceful park or along the ocean. And we've all witnessed the impact humans have had on our natural landscapes. Feng shui, however, looks more closely at this interplay by examining every detail of our living and work spaces and their relationship to our daily lives.

Each section of your home or workplace represents a part of your life. The condition of the various sectors, as well as the colors, furnishings, architectural elements, and even what's in the closets, will influence your health, career, relationships, family interactions, etc. In

Chapter 2, Looking Inside (page 29), I'll discuss how this works in more detail and show you how to analyze the different parts of your immediate personal environment.

Although the practice of feng shui involves ancient Chinese spirituality and some esoteric concepts, much of it is simply good, practical interior design. Long before most Westerners had even heard about feng shui, many successful designers were already using it because it makes sense. Here's an example: If you walked into an office and the person you'd come to see was sitting at her desk with her back to you, both of you could experience discomfort. You might feel unwelcome, and the person at the desk might be startled by your presence. Feng shui recommends positioning a desk so that the person seated behind it faces the entrance.

Feng shui also incorporates such fields as aromatherapy and the psychology of color—all with the intention of creating harmony and balance. As this ancient art continues to expand in the West, its practitioners will bring other ideas, philosophies, and disciplines into the mix and increase feng shui's effectiveness in our modern world.

The Elements of Feng Shui

To understand feng shui, you need to grasp a few basic concepts that, at first, may seem a bit strange to Westerners. But as many Asian practices such as acupuncture, yoga, and meditation gain popularity in the West, these ideas are becoming more familiar to many people here. Once you grow accustomed to viewing the world in this manner, you'll wonder how you ever saw it otherwise.

Chi

According to Chinese belief, an invisible life-force energy called chi (pronounced *kee or chee*) is present in the earth and the cosmos. Feng shui's objective, as I mentioned earlier, is to manipulate this energy so it flows smoothly through our homes, bringing us health, wealth, and happiness. Perhaps you've heard of chi in connection with Eastern medicine—acupuncturists and other healers focus on getting chi to move freely through our bodies.

You can't see chi, but you can certainly feel it. Have you ever entered a room that's been closed up for a while? It seems stale, lifeless. That's because chi isn't moving properly through the space—it's gotten stuck.

Sometimes chi moves too fast. Highways, for instance, conduct chi too rapidly and cause stress. To feel the effects of healthy chi, walk through a peaceful wooded area or sit beside a gently rippling stream. That's the impression feng shui strives to produce in our interior environments, too.

When chi gets stuck or blocked in your home, you can experience the results in a variety of ways. You may feel diminished vitality; relationships with other people might be unsatisfying or restricted; finances may be sluggish. When chi moves too quickly, you might suffer from stress; arguments or instability may damage your relationships; money may disappear as fast as you earn it.

Feng shui "cures" are designed to correct chi imbalances and direct this life-giving energy in a healthy manner so that it nourishes you and creates harmony in your home and in your life. In Part Two, Feng Shui Room by Room (page 81), I provide hundreds of quick cures you can implement in every room of your home to attract positive chi and reap its many benefits.

Yin and Yang

Feng shui also seeks to create a balance between two complementary, interdependent energies that permeate our universe. These energies are known in the East as yin (feminine) and yang (masculine). Everything in the natural and man-made worlds can be categorized as either yin or yang. It may seem a bit strange to think of inanimate objects as "feminine" or "masculine," but yin and yang aren't gender distinctions—they're energetic ones.

Yin's nature is yielding, receptive, and inner-directed—darkness, water, silence, curved shapes, and cool colors embody this force. Yang is assertive, active, and outer-oriented—we find it in light, fire, noise, sharp lines, and bright colors. Yin energy is restful; yang is stimulating. In feng shui, we attempt to combine furniture, colors, fabrics, and scents in a harmonious manner so that both types of energy are present and balanced and neither energy dominates. Too much yin can cause sluggishness; too much yang produces stress.

Try this easy exercise to analyze the yin and yang energies present in your home. On a sheet of paper, draw two columns. Head one of them "yin" and the other "yang." Now, choose a room in your home and begin listing everything you see in one or the other of these columns. Dark green sofa? Yin. Queen Anne wing chair? Yin again. High-wattage reading lamp? Yang. Killer stereo system that puts out a tidal wave of sound? Yang again. Some items combine both qualities, such as a black stove (black = yin; heat/fire = yang). See, it's not hard!

If you notice that one force predominates, you can readily offset it by adding something that contains its complementary energy. For example, a room with lots of dark furniture (yin) can be brought into balance by using yang cures, such as painting the walls a warm, bright color, or turning on more electric lights, or burning spicy incense. One of the beauties of feng shui is that it offers so many ways to rectify imbalances or to create the mood you desire. You can even fine-tune your intentions (to attract money, improve your love life, or enhance your self-image, for instance) by positioning yin or yang items in specific places in each room.

The Five Elements

Feng shui also breaks down the world into five "elemental" categories: earth, fire, water, wood, and metal. Everything in our environment, whether natural or man-made, falls into one (or more) of these categories. According to Chinese philosophy, the elements depict different aspects of chi—they represent energetic qualities, not simply physical ones.

Each element embodies specific qualities and produces a distinctive effect in your home. Earth, for instance, is stabilizing; water is fluid; fire is stimulating; and so on. Once again, the goal of feng shui is to combine the elements in your living space in a balanced, harmonious way, so that no single element predominates.

You can do an elemental analysis of your home room by room just as you did to determine its yin/yang balance. Because this can be a bit tricky at first, refer to the Elemental Table on the next page until you understand what's what.

Elemental Table

	Fire	Earth	Water	Wood	Metal
Colors	• red • orange	• brown • yellow	• black • dark blue	• green • blue	• white • gray
Materials	• electricity	• brick • stone • ceramic	• glass	• wood • paper	• metal
Shapes	• triangle	• square	• wavy • irregular	• rectangle	• round • oval
Household Objects	• candles • fireplace • stove • TV • stereo • lighting • computer • heat	• masonry • marble • tile • pottery	• sink • tub • toilet • faucets • aquarium • pool • glass items • plumbing	• plants • wood items • books	• pots & pans • silverware • appliances • metal items • metallic finishes

If you notice a room contains too much of one or two elements, you can add something from the other elemental categories to restore balance. For instance, if your home office has too much metal in it (file cabinets, metal desk, gray carpet), your business may not be growing as quickly as you'd like it to. You can remedy this problem by including fire and wood—paint the door red (fire), bring in some plants (wood), or add a rectangular bookcase (wood).

You can even emphasize or downplay certain things in your life by positioning articles from particular elemental categories in certain places. Want to turn up the heat in your love life? Put something "fire" in your bedroom's relationship area. Want to improve communication with your relatives? Add "water" items in your living room's family center. (These special areas are called *guas* in feng shui. I'll talk more about them on pages 37-38.) In Chapter 2, Looking Inside, I'll show you how to determine what goes where so you can create the results you desire.

Chapter 2
Looking Inside

As I'll show you in this chapter, much of feng shui is based on symbolic connections. But we're talking about practical connections, not some esoteric sphere here. For example, the family or living room is used for socializing, so it corresponds to your social life, family interactions, friendships, and leisure activities. The bedroom is a place for privacy, intimacy, and relaxation, so it's associated with romantic relationships and health. The home office, where work is performed, relates to money and career.

What Your Rooms Represent

Later in this chapter, I'll show you how to analyze your entire home and its individual rooms using a feng shui tool known as the *bagua* (pronounced *bah kwah*). However, the first step is to consider each room's purpose and the role it serves in your life.

If you live in a small apartment and use a room for more than one purpose, think about whether these purposes are compatible or conflicting. For instance, it's not usually a good idea to put a desk or computer in your bedroom, because work issues can interfere with rest and relaxation.

Entrance

The entrance to your home is the first thing visitors see. Therefore, it is akin to their first impression of you—the face you show the world, the public image you portray to others. Have you ever noticed how mansions and important government buildings often feature impressive entrances? These entrances immediately convey a sense of importance. What does your home's entrance say about you? What would you like it to say?

Living or Family Room

The living or family room is the part of the home where the occupants tend to come together to socialize. It is also where you entertain guests. Therefore, this room is connected with your social life, friendships, and family relationships. Because this is usually the "main" room in the home, it also influences your overall happiness and sense of well-being. Does your home include a formal living room as well as a family room? If so, these rooms play different roles and represent different facets of your life, according to how you use them.

Kitchen

Because meals are prepared in the kitchen, this room symbolizes nourishment on many levels for the home's inhabitants. From the perspective of feng shui, the kitchen—particularly the stove—is also connected with your prosperity. Therefore, its condition reveals a great deal about your financial situation. Many small homes and apartments don't have dining rooms, and their kitchens function as dining rooms, too. If this is the case in your home, consider the dining room's symbolism in conjunction with the kitchen's.

Dining Room

Usually located between the kitchen and the living room, the dining room combines the qualities of both. This is where we nourish ourselves and interact socially. From the perspective of feng shui, the dining room's condition provides clues to understanding your social life, your family relationships, and your finances. The dining room also has an effect on your health, because food is consumed and digested here.

Master Bedroom

We spend about one-third of our lives in our bedrooms, so it's no surprise that these rooms have a profound impact on us. A bedroom reveals a great deal about the person who sleeps there—particularly regarding his or her private life, because the bedroom is the place where private, intimate activities (sleeping, dressing, making love) occur. The bedroom is also linked to health, for this is where we retreat each night to rest, relax, and renew ourselves. As you might suspect, the master bedroom describes the principal adult resident(s) of the home.

Kids' Rooms

Children's bedrooms reveal their occupants' personalities, concerns, strengths, weaknesses, and pertinent issues. They also have an important connection with children's health.

Bathrooms

The bathroom—and your home's plumbing system—correspond to your elimination system. Personal cleansing rituals are performed here and wastes are flushed away. A place for purification, the bathroom is also linked with your health. If your home has more than one bathroom, consider who uses which bathroom and connect its symbolism to the most frequent user(s).

Home Office or Study

Home offices are becoming increasingly common as more people work out of their houses or bring work home with them. As you might expect, a study or work area in your home relates to your career and finances. According to feng shui, the condition of this room describes your attitudes toward money, your ability to attract wealth, your career goals, and your overall work situation.

Attic

From the perspective of feng shui, the attic symbolizes the mind and your thinking processes. It also has some bearing on your spiritual life. The attic's condition and contents can affect you psychologically and even contribute to head-oriented health problems.

Basement

The basement corresponds to the subconscious, the past, and your sense of security. Many of us have a tendency to stash stuff we don't want to deal with in the basement—in much the same way as we may keep old psychological issues stored in the subconscious.

Garage

The garage is your car's "home." In Western culture, the car symbolizes freedom and mobility. If your garage does double duty—as a workshop, for instance—consider the dual roles when you analyze your garage.

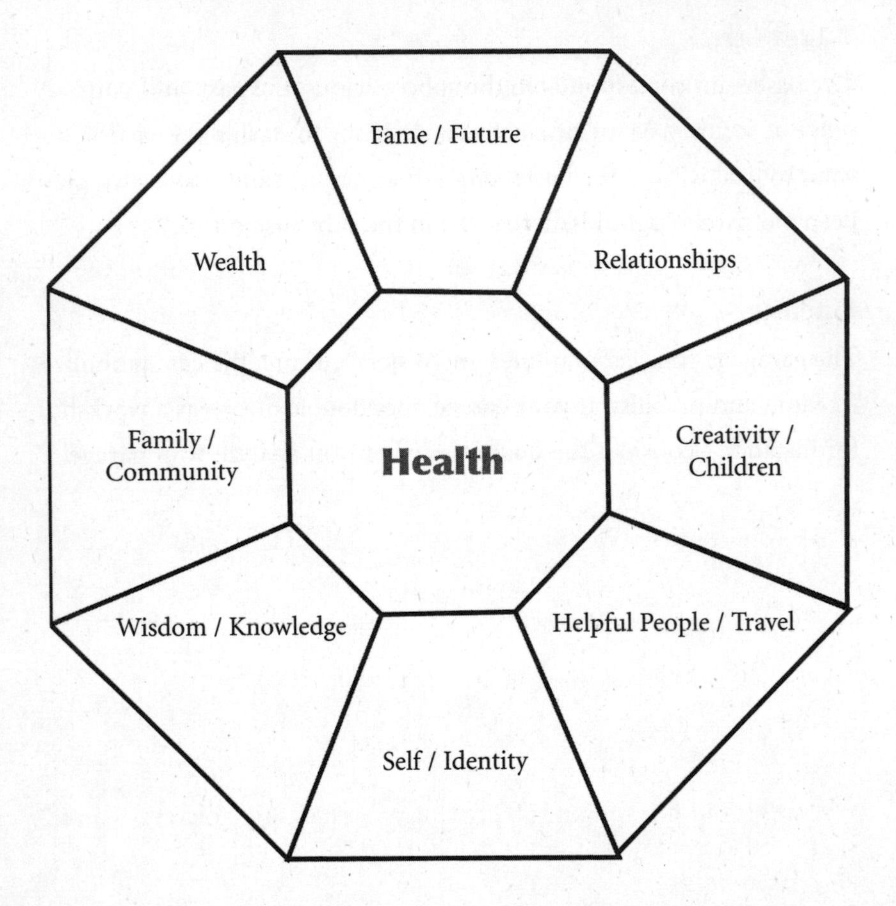
Fame / Future
Wealth
Relationships
Family / Community
Health
Creativity / Children
Wisdom / Knowledge
Helpful People / Travel
Self / Identity

The Bagua

Here in the West, some of the most popular forms of feng shui use an octagon-shaped tool called the bagua to analyze a building's interior. By superimposing a bagua over the floor plan of your home, you can quickly determine the relationship between your living space and your life.

As you can see in this diagram, the bagua is divided into nine sectors, called *gua* (pronounced *kwah*). Each gua corresponds to a different facet of your life as follows:

- **Self/Identity:** Your self-image, sense of identity, and purpose in life
- **Wisdom/Knowledge:** Your spiritual path, attitude toward knowledge, and how you learn and share information
- **Family/Community:** Your parents, extended family, heritage, neighbors, and community
- **Wealth:** Your finances and ability to earn, attract, and hold on to money

- **Fame/Future:** Your public image, career, and future goals and potential, and how you project yourself in the world

- **Relationships:** Marriage or romantic partner(s), your attitude toward love and relationships, interactions with a partner(s)

- **Creativity/Children:** Children of the mind or body, self-expression, creative endeavors, and fruitfulness

- **Helpful People/Travel:** Friends, associates, support network (including doctors, attorneys, accountants, mechanics, etc.), colleagues, clients, and travel

- **Health:** The residents' physical well-being or health-oriented challenges

Using the Bagua

Some schools of feng shui recommend using your home's front door as the starting point when analyzing your living space with the bagua. I prefer to begin with the entrance you and household members use most often, which may be a side or back door, or even an entryway through a garage. Chi (life-force energy) enters your home the same way you do—through the door—so the door you use most often is the one that conducts the greatest amount of chi into your dwelling.

If you live in an apartment building, the door to your apartment is more important to feng shui than the main entrance to the building. The main entrance is associated with all of the building's residents, but your door only pertains to those who live in your apartment.

Align the arrow on the bagua with the wall in which this door is placed, so that the octagon is positioned over your home's footprint. You can do this in your mind's eye or actually lay a bagua over a drawing of your home's floor plan. Your entrance will fall in the Self/Identity Gua, Wisdom/Knowledge Gua, or Helpful People/Travel Gua. Now you can see which gua corresponds to which room or area of your home.

Stand at the most-used entrance to your home, facing in, and mentally superimpose the bagua over your home's floor plan. The far left section is linked with wealth and financial pursuits. The far right segment describes your primary partnership and how you handle

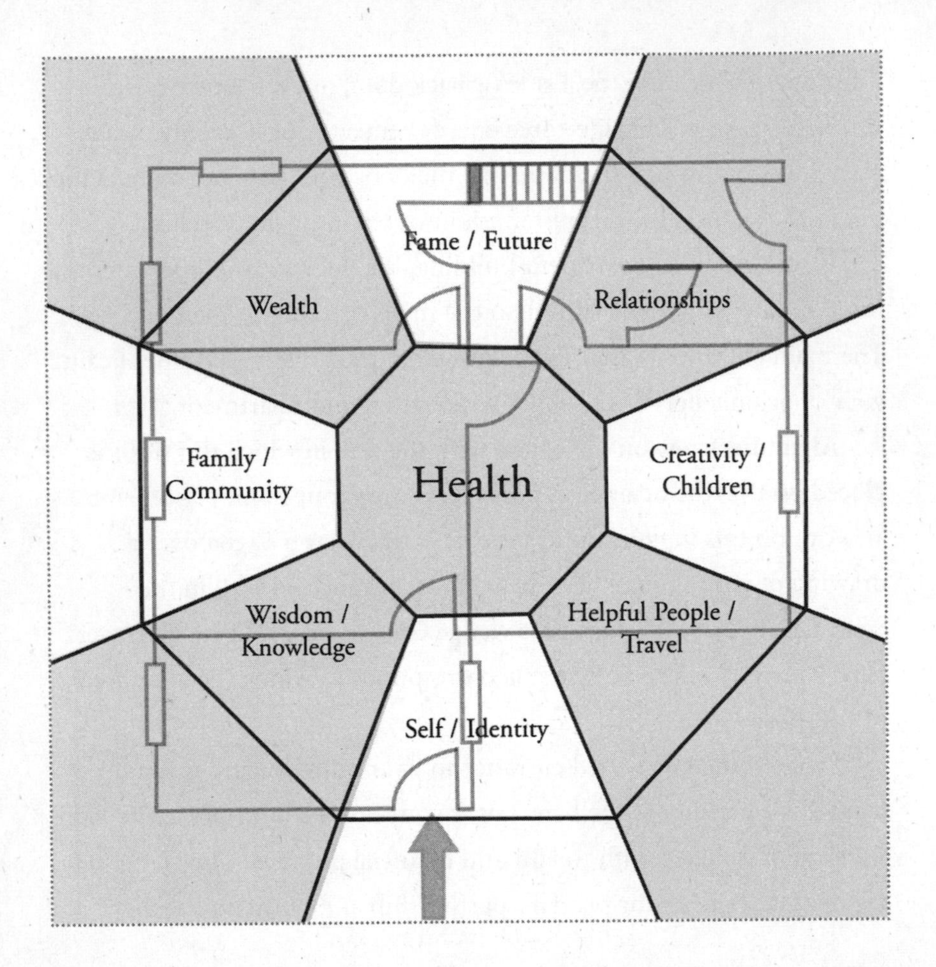
Fame / Future
Wealth
Relationships
Family / Community
Health
Creativity / Children
Wisdom / Knowledge
Helpful People / Travel
Self / Identity

romantic relationships. The area to your right corresponds to friends, associates, and helpers, and also pertains to travel. The center of your home influences your health, and so on.

Now, imagine chi traveling through your home, energizing all the different areas. Remember, chi moves pretty much the same way you do—if you can walk comfortably from room to room, chi will be able to flow smoothly, too. But if you have to sidestep furniture, clutter, or other obstacles, chi will have trouble getting around your home as well.

Try to sense the vibrations in the various parts of your living space. Are you drawn to certain spots? Do you tend to avoid others? Do you feel content in some rooms but uneasy in others? Are there certain things that annoy you? Pay attention to your intuition—the more you can connect with it and trust it, the more adept you'll become at using feng shui cures to remedy problems in your home.

Missing Guas

Unless your home is a perfect square, rectangle, circle, or octagon, you may be missing a gua or part of a gua. L-shaped and T-shaped buildings may lack two or more guas. Usually this means that the part of your life that's associated with the missing gua is inactive, problematic, or unimportant to you. If the Wealth Gua is missing, for instance, you might experience financial lack; if the Relationships Gua isn't there, you may have trouble finding a mate or maintaining a happy partnership. Fortunately, feng shui provides cures for just about every irregularity, including missing gua.

The objective is to fill in the gap so that all areas of your life are incorporated into the layout of your home. You may be able to remedy a deficiency by adding a deck, patio, garden, or fence to complete the missing sector. If that's not possible, you can create what's called a "symbolic corner." Here's how:

Using your imagination, extend the lines of your home to a point where they would join if walls actually existed. Place something attractive and eye—catching at this spot-a large plant, light, flagpole, statue, bench, or birdbath—to symbolically expand and complete your home's footprint.

Recently I worked with a woman whose home lacked a Relationships Gua. I wasn't surprised to learn that she'd been alone for a number of years. After we located her symbolic corner, she created a lovely garden spot there with a small goldfish pond surrounded by attractive plants, two handsome wooden lawn chairs, and a round table. Less than a month later, my client met her current partner.

What if you live in an apartment and can't make major changes in the building's structure? How can you remedy a missing gua if you can't tear down walls or add on to your living space?

Many feng shui cures rely on symbolism and illusion. In this case, you can symbolically "cut holes" in any walls that break up your living area or cause obstructions. Hang mirrors on the walls that currently cut off the gua—this allows you to open up the area visually and symbolically expand your apartment beyond its physical limitations. The mirrors act as substitute windows. (Even small mirrors will work—it's the principle, not the size, that matters.) You can also create the illusion of distance by hanging pictures of landscapes with faraway views on the intruding walls.

Hang mirrors to symbolically "cut through" walls that cut off a gua. You can choose mirrors of any size.

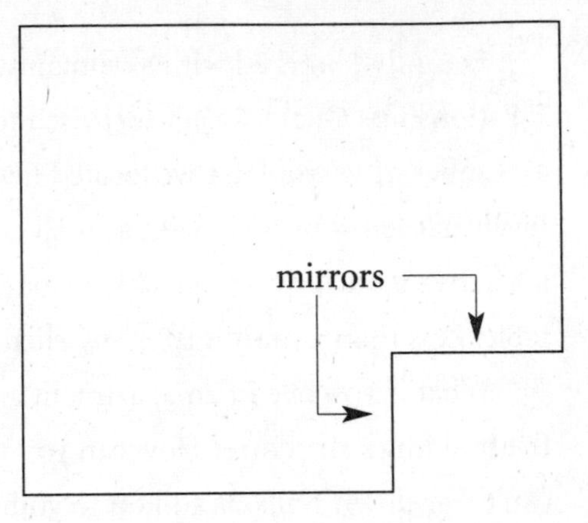

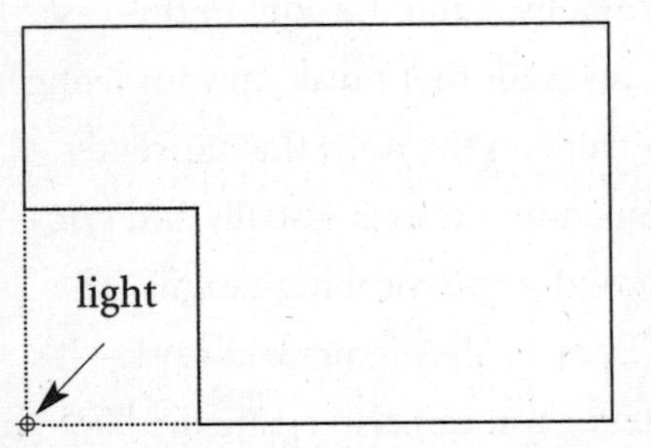

Place an outdoor light to "fill in" the missing corner of an L-shaped building. You can also plant a tree to achieve the same effect.

Using the Bagua to Analyze Each Room in Your Home

You can also use the bagua to analyze each room in your home. This technique allows you to fine-tune your intentions and bring every room in your house or apartment into balance. As you go about applying feng shui cures to the individual rooms, keep two things in mind: the room's purpose (and its symbolic associations, as described on pages 30-35) and the meanings of the guas as they pertain to the room's layout. Problems such as missing guas, slanted ceilings, and architectural obstructions will need to be corrected in each room as well as in the main footprint of your home.

Position the bagua so that the arrow lines up with the entrance to the room (or the wall in which this entrance is placed). The nine guas will align with the various sections of the room. Now you can see how each room is influencing your life and how you can make adjustments to alter any conditions you don't like.

For best results, the feng shui remedies you implement in the individual rooms should reiterate and reinforce those you've put into place in your home's overall plan (after you've determined these with the bagua). Let's say, for example, your goal is to improve your financial situation. First, identify the main Wealth Gua in your home (by aligning the bagua with your most frequently used entrance). Next, find the Wealth Gua in your kitchen, living room, and home office (if you have one). Correct any problems that may be interfering with your prosperity in all these guas so that you send out a clear, unified message.

When I bought my current home, the main Wealth Gua was missing. I quickly built a deck to fill in the missing sector, so my finances wouldn't languish. Because I work at home, I also needed to pay special attention to my office space in order to reinforce my intention to make money. I positioned my computer on a wooden desk in the office's Wealth Gua and made sure the gua was well lit to boost my chances of attracting wealth. Last, but not least, I had my stove installed in the Wealth Gua of my kitchen to help generate prosperity.

As you begin analyzing the different rooms of your home, you'll probably start to notice how accurately the condition of each gua describes your life situation. For instance, a couple I know has floor-to-ceiling bookcases in the Relationships Gua of their living room. Their relationship emphasizes intellectual pursuits, communication, and sharing ideas. Another friend's living room features a fireplace in the Family/Community Gua. She entertains often and enjoys many warm, lively interactions with relatives and neighbors.

Once you've ascertained which areas need work and what changes you'd like to bring about, turn to Part Two, Feng Shui Room by Room (page 81), and read the tips and suggestions for the areas you want to adjust. As you become more familiar with feng shui, you'll be able to design your own cures to create the circumstances you desire.

But first, let's turn to Chapter 3, Fix Your Home, Fix Your Life, and talk about how to get started.

Chapter 3

Fix Your Home, Fix Your Life

Feng shui is not a spectator sport—it's interactive and participatory. Like most things in life, the more you put into it, the more you'll get back. But that doesn't mean you have to spend a lot of money or make major alterations in your home to reap feng shui's benefits—many of the cures offered in Part Two, Feng Shui Room by Room, are inexpensive and easy to do.

It does mean you'll have to look at yourself, your life, and your home honestly—in a way you may never have done before—and be willing to confront problem areas in order to create a happier, healthier, more harmonious existence. Although this sounds appealing, be aware that some of the issues you uncover may be long-standing and deep-seated. Implementing physical changes might seem easy, but the process could require you to address some psychological matters candidly and realistically.

Go slow—make a few changes at a time, and then wait a week or so to see what happens before proceeding. Too many changes all at once can cause stress. Don't berate yourself if you backslide occasionally into old, familiar habits or patterns. It may take a while before you feel comfortable using bright colors in your Self/Identity Gua or grow accustomed to keeping your Relationships Gua uncluttered. However, applying feng shui cures demonstrates a willingness to deal with problems and can actually help you change old behaviors, attitudes, and situations in your life permanently.

Assessing Your Home

Before you begin implementing feng shui cures, I recommend doing an in-depth study or assessment of your home, room by room, to determine how the different areas of your life are being affected by your living space—and vice versa. Use one sheet of paper for each room. On each sheet of paper, list the nine sectors shown on the bagua: Self/Identity, Wisdom/Knowledge, Family/Community, Wealth, Fame/Future, Relationships, Creativity/Children, Helpful People/Travel and Health.

Start with your living room and write down what you see in each sector: furnishings, colors, architectural features, shapes, materials, artwork, lighting, and electrical equipment. Are any areas cluttered? Do any guas contain broken or malfunctioning items? Are any elemental categories lacking or underrepresented? Do any elements predominate? As you examine the contents and condition of your living room, you'll begin to see a picture of yourself emerge. Are you content with this picture, or are there things about it that you'd like to change?

Repeat this process with all the rooms of your home. As you analyze the results, keep in mind each room's symbolic meaning as well as the meanings of the individual guas. Also start thinking about the problems you'd like to correct using feng shui cures.

Popular Feng Shui Cures

Much of feng shui involves the application of carefully chosen cures. There are four types of cures that serve four basic purposes:

1. **Activating cures** break up blocked energies, stimulate the flow of chi, and encourage change. Fans, wind chimes, and mobiles fall into this category. Electrical equipment—stoves, TVs, computers, stereos, bright lights—also can be used to activate or direct chi. So can sound cures such as bells, chimes, gongs, or music. Triangles, fire colors, odd numbers, and spicy scents will stimulate chi, too.

2. **Stabilizing cures** retard the movement of chi or focus it in a particular area. Heavy objects such as stones, statuary, or large pieces of furniture can be used to stabilize chi. Squares, even numbers, and earth and metal colors will also slow down chi.

3. **Unblocking cures** remove obstacles that can interfere with the smooth movement of chi through your home. Clearing away clutter, rearranging furniture, and eliminating obstructions in your home's traffic patterns are the most common unblocking cures. Burning incense gets rid of atmospheric clutter and cleanses the air of energetic interferences.

4. **Augmenting cures** increase the amount of chi in a certain area and strengthen its beneficial effects. Their primary purpose is to promote growth. Plants, lights, crystals, and mirrors are among the most popular augmenting cures. You can also use rectangles or colors and fabrics that correspond to the wood element to enhance chi and encourage expansion.

The number and variety of feng shui cures is practically endless, limited only by your imagination. One reason feng shui has become so popular is that it offers a remedy for virtually every problem. The cures in Part Two, Feng Shui Room by Room, span all of these categories. Some even serve more than one purpose simultaneously.

As you become familiar with feng shui, you'll learn to design your own original cures to suit your personal needs.

Interior Decorating and Feng Shui

Establishing good traffic patterns throughout your home is a basic and crucial part of good interior design. It's also essential in feng shui. Remember, chi moves about your living space in pretty much the same manner you do. Take a walk through your home and pay attention to the traffic patterns in each room. Open the doors and windows. Can you get from place to place easily, or do you encounter obstacles along the way?

The first step is to clear the passageways in your home to make sure chi (and people) can access all areas without interference. After you've cleaned up clutter, fixed broken or damaged articles, and rearranged furnishings so you can move easily about your home, you're ready to progress to the finer points of interior decorating with feng shui.

Colors in Feng Shui

"Color inspires emotion," explains Master Lin Yun, one of the foremost feng shui authorities in the West, and that may be why color plays a leading role in feng shui's many cures. In China, colors are linked with the four directions, the nine sectors of the bagua, the parts of the body, the planets, and the elements. In their book, *Living Color*, Master Lin Yun and Sarah Rossback propose these colors "symbolically imitate on earth the Chinese vision of a cosmic order, and thus ensure stability, harmony, and good fortune."

Studies show that we respond in measurable ways to colors, whether we realize it or not. When test subjects are seated in a red room, their body temperature, heart rate, and respiration increase, and the subjects tend to overestimate the amount of time they've been in the room. By contrast, people placed in a blue room become more relaxed. Temperature, heart rate, and respiration slow. These subjects usually underestimate the length of time they've been in the blue room.

The Chinese consider red, black, yellow, blue, green, and white to be the six "true colors." The Western color spectrum contains the seven hues of the rainbow: red, orange, yellow, green, blue, indigo, and violet.

All of us have color preferences, some of them culturally based, some of them personal. In feng shui, however, color is used to produce specific results, as well as for aesthetic reasons. As you go about implementing feng shui cures—in your home's main gua or in a particular room—keep the following color associations in mind.

Red

In both Eastern and Western cultures, red is associated with the fire element. In China, red is considered a lucky color and is believed to attract happiness and repel harm. Gifts of money are given in red envelopes at weddings and on the Chinese New Year to bring good fortune. Requests for healing, prosperity, and other blessings are frequently written in red ink. Many feng shui cures use red ribbons, and brides traditionally wear red.

In the West, red symbolizes strength, assertiveness, and passion.

A stimulating color, red is a good choice for rooms where activity takes place, such as exercise areas or kitchens. However, it may be too strong for bedrooms and areas designated for rest & relaxation.

Put something red in any gua to activate or energize conditions associated with that gua. If your goal is to spice up a romantic partnership, for instance, use red in the Relationships Gua. If you want to strengthen your self-confidence, include red in your Self/Identity Gua. If you feel restless and would like to take a trip, add some red to your Helpful People/Travel Gua.

Orange

In China, orange is considered fortunate. A fire color, orange combines red with yellow and contains characteristics of both—the happiness of red plus the power of yellow.

In the West, we connect orange with warmth, vitality, and enthusiasm—it reminds us of fire and the sun. Orange is a stimulating color, although its variations—peach, coral, and russet—tend to be less arousing than the true hue. Packagers often choose orange for snack-food containers because it stimulates the appetite—a quality that makes orange tones ideal for kitchens and dining rooms.

Use orange to balance an area that's too yin, such as a bathroom, or to warm up a cold, dark room. To ignite your career or encourage fame, put something orange in your Fame/Future Gua. To attract lively, energetic friends, include orange in your Helpful People/Travel Gua.

Yellow

Chinese palaces were painted yellow because this color is connected with authority. Linked with the earth element and the center of the bagua, yellow represents a concentration of power and security.

In the West, we associate yellow with the sun, so it's a good choice for dark, cold rooms or hallways that lack windows. Psychologically, yellow encourages optimism and cheerfulness, so you can't go wrong using it in social areas such as living and dining rooms, kitchens, and dens. Yellow is also believed to boost creativity, and it's often a favorite of artists.

Because golden tones symbolize wealth, consider using yellow in your Wealth Gua to encourage prosperity. Yellow placed in the Creativity/Children Gua can inspire artistic tendencies and fire up your imagination. Want a sunny future? Put something yellow in your Fame/Future Gua.

Green

We associate green with spring, new life, and growth because it's the color of healthy plants. In the Chinese elemental system, it corresponds to the wood element, which promotes expansion. For these reasons, green is linked with hope and fertility. Many vegetables are green, too; therefore, this color reminds us of nutrition and health—notice how often green is used in medical facilities and worn by health-care practitioners.

A calming, yin color, green is a good choice for bedrooms, offices, and places where serenity and concentration are desired. It's also ideal for kitchens and dining rooms because it complements most foods.

In some countries, green is the color of money—use it in your Wealth Gua to attract prosperity. To encourage pleasant, peaceful interactions with relatives and neighbors, put something green in your Family/Community Gua. Include green in your Health Gua to promote balance and well-being in body, mind, and spirit.

Blue

This primary hue reminds us of water and the sky. A soothing, restful yin color, blue can help counteract stress or cool down a sunny, south-facing room. In China, blue has associations with mourning; however, in feng shui, it's considered a "wood" color and therefore is connected with growth.

Blue is a favorite color of most Westerners, perhaps because our lifestyles are so busy and stressful that we are subconsciously drawn to its restful properties. Religious art in the West often uses blue to symbolize peace.

Use blue in areas where calm or concentration is sought, such as bedrooms, offices, and meditation areas. Because we associate light blue with peace and purity and dark blue with seriousness, put something blue in your Wisdom/Knowledge Gua to improve focus, mental clarity, and memory. When used in children's bedrooms, blue helps subdue hyperactivity and sibling rivalry.

Purple

In many cultures, purple has long been connected with nobility and authority, in both secular and spiritual circles. Ancient rulers were the only people who wore "royal purple" clothing because the dye was prohibitively expensive. The Chinese use the term "purple chi" to refer to someone who is highly respected and very fortunate.

Purple is also linked with the crown chakra, an energy center located at the top of the head that serves as a receptor for higher knowledge. Consequently, people who aren't spiritually oriented may not feel comfortable wearing this powerful color. A mix of red and blue, purple combines passion with dignity, and vitality with serenity, to produce wisdom and mastery.

To attract abundance, use purple in your Wealth Gua. To improve your social standing or advance your career, place something purple in your Fame/Future Gua. To intensify the emotion and intensity in a romantic partnership, include purple in your Relationships Gua. To increase your knowledge or improve your connection with the higher worlds, add purple to your Wisdom/Knowledge Gua.

Pink

We associate pink with love and romance. Psychological studies show that people exposed to this color tend to feel more sociable and congenial. Pink has even been used in prisons to reduce violence and aggression.

In the West, pink is usually thought of as a feminine color, and few men rank it high on their list of favorites. Yet pink, a lighter shade of red, is linked with joy, good luck, harmony, and optimism. We speak of a healthy person as being "in the pink," and the positive feelings this color sparks may indeed contribute to overall well-being.

Because pink encourages friendliness, happiness, and affectionate feelings, it's an ideal color to use in social areas. To improve your love life, add pink to your Relationships Gua (I painted my entire bedroom a luscious shade of fuchsia). To attract amicable friends and encourage harmonious relationships with colleagues or clients, put something pink in your Helpful People/Travel Gua. Add pink to children's bedrooms to encourage cooperation and congeniality.

Black

Black is a dichotomy, an enigma. When we think of black in terms of light, it signifies absence, but black pigment contains all the other colors. The Chinese connect black with wealth. A "water" color in feng shui, black encourages flexibility, receptivity, and cooperation.

In the West, we associate black with mourning. But it's also the color of mystery, seriousness, and dignity, worn on formal occasions as well as by authority figures such as judges and priests. Artists and magical practitioners frequently wear black both to shield them from unwanted ambient vibrations and to incorporate all the hues of the visible spectrum into their personal space.

Black is one of the best colors to include in your Wealth Gua if you want to improve your financial prospects. It's also a good choice for your Wisdom/Knowledge Gua, where it promotes intellectual depth, concentration, and intuitive insight.

Brown

An "earth" color in both Eastern and Western systems, brown reminds us of soil, tree trunks, and stones; thus, it connotes stability and permanence. Darker shades convey a sense of dignity and timelessness; lighter shades—tan and beige—suggest freshness, adaptability, and simplicity.

Use brown in your Family/Community Gua to help you attract respect from relatives and neighbors. In your Wealth Gua, brown can help secure your finances. Put something brown in your Health Gua to promote physical strength, endurance, and longevity.

White

Like black, white is a color of opposites: White light contains all the colors of the rainbow, but white pigment represents the absence of color. In China, white is considered a color of mourning. Feng shui places it in the "metal" elemental category and links it with strength, structure, and permanence.

In the West, white symbolizes purity. Brides and holy figures wear it to show they haven't been compromised in the physical realm. White is also a color of protection and clarity in magical and mystical societies.

To improve concentration, clarity, and determination, use white in your Wisdom/Knowledge Gua. To stabilize your financial assets or limit expenditures, put something white in your Wealth Gua. White in a child's bedroom can help establish structure, discipline, and mental focus.

Gray

According to the Chinese elemental system, gray is a "metal" color, associated with structure and permanence. It also blends black and white, thereby suggesting balance, compromise, or resolution.

In the West, we speak of "gray" areas or states of ambiguity. Gray connotes something not quite pure—shady or cloudy, perhaps, but not truly grim or menacing. Gray has many degrees, from silver to charcoal, each conveying a level of seriousness, intensity, or gloom. On a positive note, gray is linked with age and wisdom, suggesting stability, calm, practicality, and dignity.

To secure your finances or encourage pragmatism in money matters, use gray in your Wealth Gua. Placed in your Wisdom/Knowledge Gua, gray can increase your ability to focus and retain information. Use gray in your Self/Identity Gua if you want to appear more stable, respectable, and dependable.

Color and the Five Chinese Elements

Fire = Red, orange

Water = Black, dark blue

Earth = Yellow, brown

Wood = Green, blue

Metal = White, gray

Shapes in Feng Shui

Shapes play an important role in interior design and in feng shui, too. Sacred geometry teaches us that each shape embodies a unique energy pattern, which is why we respond subconsciously to the shapes in our environments even if we aren't aware of doing so. Geometric shapes also possess symbolic associations, often signifying the same thing in different cultures around the world and in different eras. The circle, for instance, is a universal symbol of unity and wholeness, while the star is a symbol of hope.

The Symbolism of Shapes

Circle = Wholeness, continuity, unity, harmony, heaven

Square = Solidity, permanence, stability, earth

Triangle = Movement, change, direction toward a goal

Rectangle = Growth, expansion

Curved or wavy lines = Flexibility, interaction, fluidity

Straight lines = Rapid movement, one-pointedness

In feng shui, we intentionally use shapes to produce results.

If you refer to the Elemental Table in Chapter 1, How Feng Shui Can Help You (page 26), you'll see that each shape relates to one of the five Chinese elements. For instance, rectangles fall into in the "wood" category; therefore, a company might choose to place a rectangular conference table in its boardroom to increase business and profits. In your own home, however, you may prefer to eat from a round dining table to promote harmony among household members.

Let's take another look at the interior of your home, this time paying attention to the various shapes that show up in your furnishings, architectural features, accessories, patterns in fabrics, and more. Notice which guas include which shapes. Do any shapes predominate? Are any absent or underrepresented? What do these shapes say about you and the different areas of your life?

A man I know used to live in an apartment that had lots of sharp angles—especially in the master bedroom and in the main Relationships Gua. It's no surprise that he frequently argued with his romantic partner. When I visited the home of a professor who was having trouble advancing in her career, I immediately noticed that her Fame/Future Gua contained mostly curved forms and wavy lines, which revealed her tendency to be too cooperative and indecisive. Soon after she positioned a large rectangular bookcase in that sector, she received a promotion.

Usually, the goal of feng shui is to create balance. Try to combine shapes throughout your home so that none overpowers the others. Make sure each room contains things that represent each shape, in relatively equal portions. Some pieces of furniture may be composed of more than one shape. For instance, a wing chair is made up mainly of curved shapes, but if it's upholstered with a flame-patterned fabric, you've got triangles there as well.

You may decide to emphasize one or two shapes in a room or gua to produce a specific result. Many circles and curves placed in the Relationships Gua of your master bedroom, for instance, will encourage harmony in a romantic partnership. Squares in your Wealth Gua will serve to stabilize your finances. Triangles in your Fame/Future Gua can stimulate your career or direct you toward a particular goal.

Numbers in Feng Shui

Numbers are more than simply units of measurement—they contain mystical and symbolic meanings, too. In fact, numbers are probably the most frequently used symbols in our daily lives—our Social Security numbers, birth dates, phone numbers, credit card numbers, and street addresses. The ancient Greek philosopher Pythagoras, considered to be the father of mathematics, believed numbers signified universal principles and that the world could be interpreted and understood through numbers.

Think about some of the expressions we use that include numbers. "One-pointed" means someone is focused on a specific goal and is not likely to be swayed by other people. "Four-square" describes a person who is solid, dependable, honest, and stable. "The whole nine yards" indicates completion, the ultimate, all there is. Without realizing it, we've incorporated the hidden meanings of numbers into these sayings.

Like shapes, numbers possess certain energetic qualities that feng shui can tap to produce desired results. Several years ago, I decided to make some changes in my life path. On the wall in my Fame/Future Gua, I hung three paintings that depicted goals I wished to achieve. Within a matter of weeks, my entire life began to shift, and within a few months I'd undergone a significant transformation.

Many people have "lucky numbers." In feng shui, the number 3 and its multiples 6 and 9 are considered lucky. Consequently, many feng shui cures tap into the positive energies of these numbers. The *I Ching*, China's 3,000-year-old spiritual and philosophical text, uses trigrams, or three-line patterns, to symbolize universal energies. This ancient oracle includes 64 different six-line configurations called hexagrams, each made up of two trigrams, to provide guidance. The bagua contains nine sectors, and each sector corresponds to one of these trigrams.

In some instances, the meanings of shapes and numbers overlap—a square has four corners, and both the shape and the number embody similar energies. If you can't use a certain shape in a particular part of your home's interior, you may be able to substitute the corresponding number instead. Part Two, Feng Shui Room by Room, includes lots of easy ways to use numbers in your feng shui decorating process.

Numbers and Their Meanings

0 = Unity, wholeness, harmony, continuity

1 = Beginnings, the individual

2 = Polarity, pairing, complementary forces

3 = Creativity, growth, movement toward a goal

4 = Stability, permanence

5 = Change, activity, instability

6 = Cooperation, give-and-take

7 = Withdrawal, introspection

8 = Money, business, material power

9 = Fulfillment, completion

Materials in Feng Shui

The Elemental Table in Chapter 1, How Feng Shui Can Help You (page 26), lists many materials and their elemental correspondences. Brick, for instance, comes under the "earth" heading. In addition to the obvious relationships (e.g., wood = wood, metal = metal), you can choose to decorate with certain textures and fibers to bring in the elemental energies you desire or to balance other factors (such as shapes and colors).

Smooth, sleek fabrics such as silk and rayon are considered "water" materials. Thick, plush, or coarse fabrics, such as wool, nubby cotton, and velvet, fall into the "earth" category. Rattan, straw, paper, and cane can be classified as "wood." Shiny, metallic fibers correspond to the "metal" element.

When you use soft, fluffy materials such as flannel, goose down, or lamb's wool in a bedroom, you establish the sense of comfort and security associated with the earth element. Baskets can help offset the preponderance of water and metal energies in a bathroom. Silk, a "water" material, enhances cooperation when placed in the Relationships Gua, while simultaneously creating a symbolic association with elegance and sensuality.

Scents in Feng Shui

For thousands of years, aromatic oils, gums, and resins have been used for medicinal and cosmetic purposes, as well as in sacred rituals. Ancient Chinese texts describe the therapeutic, philosophical, and spiritual properties of aromatics. The Bible discusses special oils for anointing and healing. The Egyptians raised the use of perfumes and scented oils to an art form, employing them in all areas of life, from seduction to embalming.

Several millennia later, aromatherapy has once again come into its own. When inhaled, scents affect the limbic system of the brain, the portion associated with memory, emotions, and libido. That is why certain smells have the ability to reawaken long-ago memories. The brain responds instantly to odors, and shifts in brainwave function can be measured immediately after a person sniffs a certain scent. Because aromatic substances—incense, scented candles, essential oils, perfumes, and potpourri—interact with the body both physiologically and psychologically, they have a wide variety of beneficial applications in feng shui.

Sage, for instance, has long been used in many cultures to clear the air and dispel "stuck" chi. Mint, clove, cinnamon, cedar, geranium, lemon, and eucalyptus are stimulating scents. Use peppermint, cinnamon, or cedar in your Wealth Gua to increase your money-making prospects or in your Fame/Future Gua to jump-start your career. Vanilla, lavender, sweet orange, and chamomile have a calming effect on us—use these aromas in the Family/Community Gua to ease tensions with relatives or neighbors. Rose, ylang-ylang, musk, patchouli, bergamot, and jasmine are known for their aphrodisiac qualities—in your Relationships Gua, these scents can add spice to your love life.

Images in Feng Shui

As artists, advertisers, politicians, spiritual leaders, and occultists know, images trigger subconscious associations for us and serve as psychological motivators. When we view a picture, a symbol, or an icon, we instantly make certain connections. A trophy connotes success. A Rolls Royce symbolizes wealth. A heart represents love.

Because we respond in powerful and predictable ways to images, they are among feng shui's most important cures. Some symbols are personal or cultural; others are universal. A woman I know used to have a painting of a peaceful landscape hanging in her Helpful

People/Travel Gua. Although the picture was quite beautiful, it lacked people or activity. I suggested moving it to her Health Gua, where its calming symbolism helped relieve stress. She replaced it with a picture that showed a celebration at a cheerful café and very quickly began to meet new friends.

Although each of us makes personal associations with symbols and pictures, some images are generally considered favorable. Consequently, feng shui practitioners frequently use them as cures. See the chart on page 78 for a helpful list of images and their meanings.

Images and Their Meanings

Crane = Wisdom, longevity, fertility

Peacock = Wealth, dignity, respect

Dove = Love

Bluebird = Happiness

Phoenix = Power, luxury, rising above adversity

Spiral = Life energy

Circle = Unity, wholeness

Turtle = Protection

Stars = Hope

Sun = Clarity, life energy, happiness

Lion, tiger = Power, loyalty, leadership, protection

Dragon = Success, abundance

Flowers = Growth, beauty, love

Fish, especially goldfish (koi) = Wealth, career success

Horse = Longevity, wisdom, goodwill

Water = Nourishment, peace, cooperation

Buddha, Kwan Yin = Blessings, compassion, joy, good fortune

As you examine your home, notice the pictures and images displayed there. What messages do they convey? What feelings and impressions do they spark in you? Also check inside drawers, cabinets, and closets—even objects that aren't in view can influence the energies in a particular gua. Choose images that present the ideas you desire and that remind you of your intentions whenever you look at them.

Now that you have a good working knowledge of feng shui and how to use it in your home, it's time to get started! In Part Two, Feng Shui Room by Room, you'll find hundreds of ways to put feng shui to work for you.

Part Two

Feng Shui Room by Room

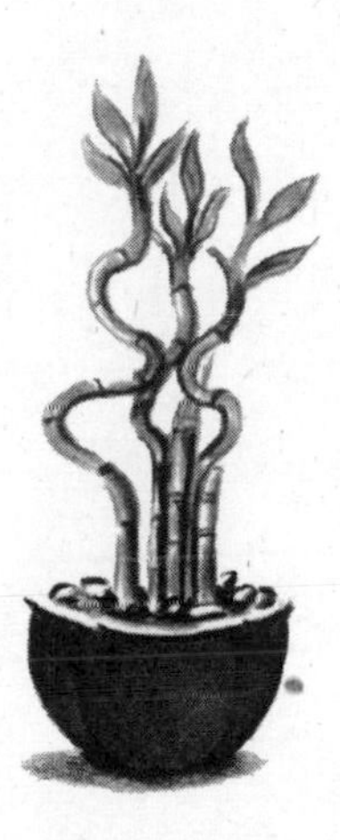

Chapter 4

First Impressions: The Entrance

Align the bagua with your driveway or sidewalk.

The area surrounding your home plays a role in your health, wealth, and happiness. You can examine your yard using the bagua, just as you did when you analyzed your home. Superimpose the bagua over a diagram or plot plan of your property by placing the octagon so the arrow lines up with the driveway, sidewalk, or other entrance to your property (see page 40). This process allows you to see which sections of the yard relate to which areas of your life so that you can correct problems as needed.

Keep your entrance area free of clutter.

Your home's entrance is the first thing passersby and visitors see—åtheir first impressions of you will be gleaned from the "face" your home shows to the world. Make sure this first impression is a good one by keeping the area free of clutter. From a practical perspective, clutter can cause accidents, too. Get kids to pick up their toys, rake leaves, and clean up litter so your home always looks its best.

Keep steps, sidewalks, porches, and decks in good repair.

This cure is both practical and symbolic. To prevent possible accidents and injuries, make sure steps, sidewalks, porches, and decks are sound and in good condition. Damage also signifies problems in other areas of your life and conveys a bad impression of you to people who see or visit your home.

Clear the walkways to your home.

To invite and direct chi into your home, clear the sidewalk, driveway, and/or other paths that lead to the building. If walkways are cluttered or obscured, chi will have a harder time reaching your home, and its life-generating energy will be diminished in the process.

Create a gently curved walkway to your home.

A curving sidewalk, path, or other walkway allows chi to flow toward your home in a pleasantly controlled manner and produces the most positive effects. A straight path, on the other hand, causes chi to rush toward your home and create tension.

Hang a bagua mirror on your door.

Hang a bagua mirror on your door so that it faces the street. The mirror will reflect back harmful energies and keep them away from your home.

Use plants to deflect "bad vibes" from the street.

If you live near a street, you may be getting zapped by "bad vibes" (known as *shar chi* in feng shui terms)—especially if your home is situated at a T-shaped intersection and cars drive directly at you. To alleviate the disruptive effects of this pattern, plant shrubs between your home and the street. They provide a visual screen and block the oncoming energies from the street.

Place a turtle near your entrance.

Turtles symbolize protection in China. Display an image of a turtle near the entrance of your home to safeguard the members of your household and your property.

Position a light in the Wealth Gua of your entry area.

Chi is drawn to light. As soon as it enters your home, focus its life-giving energy into your Wealth Gua by placing a light in this spot.

Paint your door red, peach, or purple for good luck.

Red, peach, and purple are considered lucky colors in China. Paint your front door one of these bright hues to attract chi and good fortune to your home.

Install good lighting at your home's entrance.

Chi is attracted to light, so installing adequate lighting near the entrance to your home will invite chi to bring its life-giving energy your way. From a practical standpoint, good lighting also helps you and visitors find the way to your home and can prevent accidents.

Use a fountain to disperse harmful street chi.

Here's another way to disperse stressful vibrations created by traffic: Install a fountain or birdbath between the street and your building. This cure blocks shar chi and protects your home from the tension shar chi causes.

Attach brass numerals to your front door.

Shiny brass numerals will also draw chi to your home. Affix them to your front door and remember to keep them polished.

Plant evergreen shrubs near your home's entrance.

Because evergreen shrubs don't lose their foliage in winter, they symbolize longevity, health, and prosperity. Plant holly, pine, spruce, or other evergreens near your home's entrance to attract chi and keep your entryway attractive all year long.

Make sure doors open easily.

Does your front door stick? This condition suggests that some areas in your life may be stuck, too. It also inhibits the smooth flow of chi into your home and diminishes its positive effects. Adjust or repair a sticky door promptly, and make sure clutter and obstacles inside don't prevent it from opening easily.

Keep plants neatly trimmed.

Trim shrubs and other outdoor plants periodically so they convey positive messages. Dead leaves and limbs symbolize decay. Overgrown foliage suggests your life is out of control. Healthy, well-cared for plants represent a healthy, happy living situation.

Plant red flowers in front of your home.

Because red is a lucky color in China, you can improve your good fortune by planting red flowers in front of your home. Window boxes or planters are good choices for apartment dwellers—wood containers signify growth, and ceramic or stone pots represent security.

Paint your entry area yellow to promote good cheer.

A foyer or entry area seems cheery and bright when it's painted sunny yellow. Especially in the winter or in a foyer that lacks natural sunlight, a yellow entrance makes visitors feel welcome.

Hang a photo of household members in the foyer.

This cure introduces visitors to the people who live in your home. It also gives anyone who enters your home a sense of being greeted by household members and welcomed into your living space.

Mist your entrance with an inviting scent.

To stimulate positive feelings in those who enter your home, mist your entryway with a scent that evokes a sense of security, comfort, and welcome. Vanilla is a popular choice because many people associate this warm, pleasing aroma with baking and nourishment. Pine and balsam scents spark images of festive winter holidays and good cheer. In the summer or in warmer regions, citrus scents seem clean and refreshing.

> **TIP: Consult a good book on aromatherapy to fine-tune the impressions you wish to convey with scent.**

Position a lion near your entrance.

Lions symbolize protection, power, and leadership. In China, statues of lions often are placed just outside the door to a building to safeguard it. Display a sculpture or picture of a lion near your entrance to guard your home and bring good fortune your way.

Hang a circular wreath on your door.

Present an image of harmony and hospitality to your visitors by hanging a circular wreath on your entry door. Change the wreath each season to connect the occupants of your home with the seasons and the cycles of the year.

Hang a landscape with a distant view on an obstructing wall.

Another technique for symbolically expanding a confined space is to hang a picture of a landscape with a faraway view on the obstructing wall. This image creates an illusion of openness and distance.

Place a circular bowl in your foyer.

A decorative circular bowl placed in your foyer also conveys a sense of harmony and unity to anyone who enters your home. Set the bowl in a convenient spot—on a hall table or shelf, for example—so household members and visitors can place keys, eyeglasses, gloves, cell phones, and other items in it when they come inside.

Put a plant in a ceramic container in your foyer.

Plants symbolize life and attract chi into your home. A ceramic container represents the earth element, which is associated with comfort and security.

TIP: Choose a red clay pot for good luck, or tie a red ribbon around the container.

Put a plush area rug in your entry area.

Thick, soft materials emphasize the earth element and provide a sense of security, comfort, and stability. A plush area rug in your foyer or front hall gives everyone who enters your home a warm welcome.

Illuminate your foyer adequately.

Have you ever entered a dark hallway or vestibule and felt uncomfortable even anxious? A brightly lit foyer, on the other hand, invites you to enter—visitors instantly feel safe and welcome in your home. Because chi is attracted to light, a well-illuminated foyer or entrance hall also encourages chi to come into your home.

Hang a wind chime in your entryway to circulate chi.

Another way to circulate chi is to hang a wind chime in your entryway. The pleasing sound of the chimes will break up stuck chi and allow it to move more freely into other parts of your home.

Hang a mirror on an obstructing wall.

When you enter your home, do you immediately encounter a wall? If so, you have undoubtedly experienced the sensation of being blocked or stopped by this obstruction. The same thing happens to chi when it comes into your home. To alleviate this condition, hang a mirror on the wall. The mirror symbolically cuts a hole or window in the wall, thereby opening up the confined space and allowing chi to enter more easily.

In a long hallway, use lighting to slow down chi.

If your home has a long, straight hallway that leads from the front door directly to the back, chi will rush down the hall without circulating throughout your home. To slow down chi, position lamps, ceiling lights, or wall sconces at intervals along the hall. Chi will be attracted to the lights and linger in your home, rather than rushing right out the back door.

Use accent lighting to direct chi into your home.

Once chi has entered your home, the goal is to get it to circulate throughout the interior so it energizes every room. One way to do this is with accent lighting, installed either in the ceiling or along the walls. Position lights so that one follows the other, directing chi—and people—from the foyer into the main part of your home.

Pay attention to what's reflected in a mirror.

Because mirrors reflect whatever is before them, they double the energies of objects. When you hang a mirror in your hallway, pay attention to what it reflects. In front of a mirror, position decorative items that represent qualities you desire and let the mirror "double" their benefits.

Install a ceiling fan in your entryway to circulate chi.

Sometimes chi can get stuck in a foyer or entrance hall. To circulate it into the main part of your home, install a ceiling fan in your entryway.

Hang nine pictures in a long hallway.

Like the previous cure, this one helps slow down “rushing” chi by causing it to pause and focus on each picture as it travels down the hall.

Hang an attractive picture at the beginning of an entryway staircase.

Many entrance hallways feature stairs leading up or down to another level. In layouts like this, chi tends to rush up or down the stairs, rather than circulating evenly throughout the main floor. Hang an attractive picture at the beginning of the staircase. As you enter, your attention is drawn to the picture, causing chi to pause and linger on the main floor.

Place a large stone or sculpture at the bottom of an entryway staircase.

Like the previous cure, this one prevents chi from immediately rushing up the stairs instead of flowing smoothly throughout your home. Heavy objects hold down chi and keep it on the ground floor long enough to energize this level before it ascends to the second story.

TIP: Consider displaying a jade statue of Kwan Yin, the Asian goddess of compassion, in this spot.

Clear the passageways from your foyer into your living area.

Clear away any obstructions that inhibit easy movement from the foyer to the main part of your living area. Clutter, furniture, or architectural elements that jut into the walkways will block chi and make it difficult for you to move freely into your home.

Create a focal point in your entry area.

Help chi and visitors get their bearings when they enter your home by creating an attractive focal point for them to look at, such as a large healthy plant, an appealing picture or sculpture, or a handsome piece of furniture.

Decorate your entrance with all five elements.

To establish immediately a sense of balance and harmony in your home, include all five elements in your entry area. One way to do this is to place a mirror (water) with a brass (metal) frame above a rectangular (wood) hall table and set a ceramic (earth) vase of red (fire) flowers on the table.

Display a laughing Buddha figurine in the Family/Community Gua of your entryway.

This symbol of good fortune sends blessings to all who enter your home. It also shows your intention to maintain positive relationships with family members and neighbors.

Use a triangle to direct chi into your home.

To keep chi from languishing in your foyer, position a triangle so that it points toward the main part of your home. This symbol works like an arrow to direct chi into your living area.

Put a piece of jade in your entryway's Family/Community Gua

Jade is linked with good health, prosperity, and well-being. Put a chunk of tumbled jade or, better yet, an attractive figurine made of jade in your entryway's Family/Community Gua. This cure invites good fortune to bless relatives and neighbors who come into your home.

Keep closet doors shut.

Because closets represent hidden or private matters, keep the door shut on an entry area closet. This prevents your personal affairs from becoming public.

Place six objects on a hall table.

Six is the number of give-and-take and encourages cooperation. When visitors or household members enter your home, they subconsciously register this number and its symbolism. Use objects that represent your intentions or that have positive associations for you.

Chapter 5

Social Space: The Living Room

Position sofas and chairs so no one's back faces the door.
Arrange sofas and chairs in your living room so that when seated, no one will have his or her back to the entrance. This configuration welcomes people into the room and prevents those who are already seated from being startled by someone coming up behind them.

Position furniture so it doesn't block doors or windows.

Chi enters your home via the doors and windows. If, when you open a door, you bump a piece of furniture, chi will be blocked and your social life could suffer. Arrange furniture in your living room so that it doesn't interfere with the free flow of chi.

Use a round or oval rug to encourage congeniality.

Circles are ancient, universal symbols of unity and harmony. To promote unity, peace, and happiness among family members or your social contacts, put a round or oval rug in your living room.

Use a rectangular rug to expand your social network.

In feng shui, rectangles are used to stimulate growth. If you want to expand your social network, meet new people, or encourage more interaction with friends and neighbors, place a rectangular area rug in your living room.

Use an area rug to create a sense of togetherness.

One way to strengthen symbolically the bonds among the members of your household is to place a large area rug in your living room. Make sure all the seating pieces in the room touch or rest on the rug. The rug serves as a unifying element, tying all the individual furnishings together. This decorating technique also enhances connections with friends and neighbors and can improve your social life in general.

Use peach in your living room to attract luck and love.

Peach, which combines pink with yellow (the color of optimism and creativity), is also a good choice to include in your decorating scheme. In China, peach is linked with luck in love—the term "peach blossom luck" refers to someone who easily attracts romantic partners. If your intent is to bring new companions into your life, use peach in your living room's color scheme.

Include pink in your decorating scheme to encourage sociable feelings.

Pink is the color of love and sociability, so it's an ideal color to use in the living room—or any area of your home where family members come together or where you entertain guests. Fuchsia and magenta add a note of wisdom and spirituality; reddish pink increases passion and enthusiasm.

Include dark blue or black in your decorating scheme to facilitate conversation.

According to feng shui, black and dark blue are "water" colors, which encourage adaptability and communication. Use these colors in your living room's décor if you want to stimulate lively conversations with friends and family members. Water colors will also help people be more flexible in their thinking and promote give-and-take.

TIP: Combine pink or peach with dark blue or black to create a balance of thinking and feeling in the social areas of your home.

Include yellow in your decorating scheme to encourage cheerfulness and optimism.

Especially in a room that doesn't get much natural light or in a cool, north-facing area, yellow can promote upbeat feelings and good cheer. Yellow symbolizes the sun and encourages warm, positive feelings among family members and guests. Yellow can also stimulate creativity.

TIP: The golden end of the yellow hue corresponds to money, so this is an ideal color to use if your living room happens to fall in your home's Wealth Gua. Or place something golden yellow in the Wealth Gua of your living room to attract prosperity.

Include deep green in your decorating scheme to promote serenity.

Green, a yin color that symbolizes plants, has a soothing effect on us and makes us feel calm and peaceful. The darker shades especially remind us of the shadowy depths of the forest or the ocean. To encourage a sense of serenity among friends or family members, include deep green in your living room's decorating scheme.

Use green in your living room to enhance prosperity.

Green is also the color of paper money in some cultures. In the West, we associate green with the earth element, which represents material goods and money. Including green in your decorating scheme can help increase prosperity, especially when used in the Wealth Gua of your living room.

Place a lamp in your living room's Wealth Gua.

Lamps symbolize the life-giving light of the sun and stimulate chi. Place a lamp in the Wealth Gua of your living room to enhance the chi in that area and to direct energy toward financial gains. If your goal is to stabilize your finances, choose a lamp with a metal or ceramic base. If you want to increase your prosperity, a wooden base is preferable.

Place a lamp in your living room's Fame/Future Gua.

If your goal is to ensure a bright future or you want to enhance your reputation, place a lamp in the Fame/Future Gua of your living room. A lamp with a red base can bring you good luck. A lamp with a black base can help attract prosperity.

Burn incense to clear the air.

One of the easiest ways to chase away "bad vibes" in your environment is to burn incense. After an argument or upsetting incident, burn incense scented with sage, mint, or pine to clear the air and restore peace. It's a good idea to burn incense after a party, too, to get rid of the energy left behind by other people and to restore balance in your home. You may also wish to do a daily cleansing ritual by burning incense in your living room each morning.

Burn incense to stimulate communication and congeniality.

Incense combines the Western elements of air and fire, which are linked with communication and enthusiasm respectively. In some spiritual traditions, incense is burned to send messages and prayers to deities. To attract cheerful companions with whom you can enjoy lively conversation and good times, burn incense in the Helpful People/Travel Gua of your living room regularly. Doing so demonstrates your interest in friendship and sociability.

Ring a bell to chase away bad vibes.

Here's another quick and easy clearing cure—ring a bell when you enter the living room. The pleasing sound breaks up stale energy and helps chase away bad vibes. Ring the bell once in each corner of the room and once in the center to stimulate positive chi.

Hang faceted crystal balls in dark corners.

Does your living room have some shadowy corners? These dark spots are like "black holes" that diminish the life-giving power of chi. To brighten dim corners symbolically, hang small crystal or glass balls or prisms from the ceiling, preferably from red string (for good luck).

Wash the windows in your living room.

In feng shui, windows symbolize eyes. Clean windows help you see things clearly; dirty ones can cause confusion or limit your perspective. If a situation with friends or household members is murky, wash the windows in your living room to open up your perception and give you a better perspective. Pay attention to the sector in which the window(s) are located. Wash a window in the Creativity/Children Gua to gain insight into your kids, in the Relationships Gua to understand a spouse or significant other better, and in the Helpful People/Travel Gua to improve relationships with friends, advisors, and associates.

Clean ashes from the fireplace regularly.

Ashes represent the past and things you no longer want or need in your life. Clean your fireplace or woodstove often to avoid these unwanted associations, as well as possible safety hazards.

Place six candles on the mantelpiece.

Six is the number of give-and-take and joint resources. In many homes, a fireplace or woodstove is a source of comfort and relaxation, where people sit together to socialize. By placing six candles on your mantel, you encourage positive exchanges with friends and loved ones. Symbolically, this cure also invites household members to share their possessions, experiences, abilities, and affection with one another.

Rearrange the furniture in your living room periodically.

To prevent stagnation, move the furniture in your living room around at least once each year. By changing your furniture arrangement, you symbolically invite new people and experiences into your life. You can direct the changes you wish to make by only moving pieces in a particular gua; for example, shift items in your Self/Identity Gua to stimulate personal growth.

Burn lavender-scented candles in your living room.

To encourage peaceful feelings or relaxation among friends or family members, burn candles scented with lavender or vanilla essential oils. (Note: Synthetic fragrances don't produce the same effects as pure essential oils.)

Burn spicy-scented candles in your living room.

To spark lively intellectual exchanges and stimulate enthusiasm among friends or family members, burn candles scented with spicy aromas, such as cinnamon, clove, ginger, cedar, sandalwood, or patchouli.

Burn floral-scented candles in your living room.

To promote feelings of affection and camaraderie among friends or family members, burn candles scented with essential oils of rose, gardenia, ylang-ylang, bergamot, sweet orange, or jasmine.

Display family photos in your living room.

Displaying photos of family members in your living room demonstrates your desire for congenial relationships with loved ones. Not surprisingly, the best spot to place photos of relatives is in the Family/Community Gua; the best position for pictures of friends is in the Helpful People/Travel Gua. Put pictures of children in the Creativity/Children Gua.

Place a vase of red flowers in your living room.

In China, red is considered a lucky color. To encourage good fortune in family and social matters, place a vase of red flowers in your living room. You can fine-tune this good luck by positioning the flowers in a specific gua—the Wealth Gua to attract money, the Self/Identity Gua to enhance your sense of self-esteem, or the Family/Community Gua to improve relationships with neighbors and relatives. Be sure to trim or remove flowers as soon as they start to fade.

Configure seating in "conversation groups."

Interior designers arrange sofas and chairs in "conversation groups" so that people seated there can talk to one another without shouting. Try to position seating so that no one is more than about eight feet away from anyone else. Group furniture in L, U, semicircular, or parallel configurations to facilitate conversation and camaraderie.

Place a jade Buddha in your living room.

The Buddha is a most auspicious symbol in feng shui. In both Eastern and Western traditions, jade is associated with good health, prosperity, and well-being. To attract the good things in life, place a jade Buddha—preferably a laughing Buddha—in a prominent spot in your living room.

Place an image of Kwan Yin in your living room.

Kwan Yin, the beloved goddess of compassion in many Eastern cultures, is another auspicious presence you may wish to include in your home. Place an image of her in your living room to encourage love, peace, and compassion among family members and friends.

Let a peacock bring you respect and good fortune.

In China, peacocks are viewed as symbols of respect, beauty, and good fortune. Display an image of a peacock in your living room to attract these qualities.

TIP: The best spots to place an image of a peacock are in your Self/Identity Gua or Fame/Future Gua.

Use a phoenix to increase your power.

The legendary phoenix is rich with symbolism. It represents power and triumph over adversity. Display a picture of a phoenix in your living room to help you increase personal power and remove obstacles to happiness.

Keep walkways through your living room free of clutter and obstacles.

Chi moves around your home in much the same way you do. If the passageways through your living room are obstructed by furniture or clutter, chi will have a hard time circulating. The blocked energy can adversely affect relationships with family members or friends. To keep chi moving freely and maintain open communication among loved ones, make sure the walkways through your living room are free of obstacles.

Position one eye-catching item in your Self/Identity Gua.

The living room is usually connected with social interactions, family, and friends; however, you don't want your own individuality to be eclipsed by other people. To strengthen or establish your sense of self, place a single important or eye-catching item in the Self/Identity Gua of your living room, such as a distinctive piece of furniture, a striking sculpture or painting, or an object that has special meaning for you.

Hang a picture of a landscape to create the illusion of space.

Especially in a small room, a picture of a landscape with a distant view can symbolize expansiveness and broader horizons. Also use this cure to cut symbolically an opening in a wall that blocks or intrudes into your living space. (See Chapter 3, Fix Your Home, Fix Your Life, beginning on page 49, for more information.)

Hang a picture of mountains in your living room.

A landscape that features mountains can encourage you or family members to climb higher and achieve lofty goals—the perfect symbolism to display in your living room's Fame/Future Gua.

For your living room, choose artwork that depicts people.

An empty landscape isn't the best choice for your living room. Make sure there are people in the pictures you display in the social areas of your home—otherwise, you're sending a message that you prefer a solitary existence.

Hang four pictures in your living room's Wealth Gua.

Four is the number of stability and security. To help stabilize your finances and keep money from going out faster than it comes in, hang a grouping of four pictures in your living room's Wealth Gua. Make sure the images in the pictures symbolize prosperity or abundance.

Hang three pictures in an area to stimulate change.

Is there something about your family or social life you'd like to change? One way to spark change is to hang three pictures in the gua that represents the area in which you'd like transformation to occur. Be careful, though—change isn't always easy to control. Choose pictures that represent the situations you desire.

Use rectangular wooden picture frames to promote growth.

In China, wood and rectangles are associated with expansion. To encourage growth, frame artwork and photographs in wood. If your objective is to increase your social circle, hang pictures in the Helpful People/Travel Gua. If you'd like to add to your family, place wood-framed pictures in the Creativity/Children Gua of your living room.

Use metal picture frames to strengthen or stabilize an area of your life.

If your goal is to strengthen family or social relationships or to promote stability in your home life, choose metal frames for artwork. Place pictures in the gua that represents the area in which you are seeking stability, and make sure the images in the pictures describe your intentions.

Choose furniture with curved lines to promote harmony.

Curved lines and circles are ancient, universal symbols of unity and congeniality. Feng shui considers curves to be yin. To encourage cooperation and harmony with friends or family members, choose living room furnishings with curved lines, such as French country, Queen Anne, or Victorian styles.

Use gilt frames to attract money.

Gilt (gold-colored paint) represents wealth and luxury, so use gilt frames for artwork if you want to improve your finances. Hang pictures in the Wealth Gua of your living room to attract prosperity. Remember to choose images that represent abundance and riches.

TIP: Rectangular frames encourage growth; square frames help stabilize your finances.

Place a bookcase in your living room.

If you'd like to attract intelligent, literary companions or emphasize learning and communication among family members, place a bookcase in your living room. The best place to locate it is in the living room's Family/Community Gua or Helpful People/Travel Gua.

Choose a "split-complementary" color scheme for your living room.
This popular color scheme uses three hues to attract good luck and establish a sense of harmony in your living environment. Use a color wheel that shows the primary, secondary, and tertiary colors. Select a color you like as your principal hue. Then find its "complement" (the color directly opposite it on the wheel). The two hues on either side of the complementary color are the ones to use in conjunction with your main color. For example, combine yellow (main color) with magenta and blue-violet.

Choose a color scheme that includes three hues.
Three is considered a lucky number in feng shui. For your living room, choose a decorating palette that includes three colors and use them in this ratio: about 60 percent of the main color, 30 percent of the second (complementary) color, and 10 percent of the third (accent) color.

Arrange symbols of your faith in the Wisdom/Knowledge Gua.
To attract companions who share your spiritual views, place icons, religious artwork, spiritual texts, or other symbols of your faith in the Wisdom/Knowledge Gua of your living room.

Use purple in your Wisdom/Knowledge Gua.
Purple is the color of the crown chakra, an energy center at the top of your head that serves as a link between the body and higher knowledge. It's also a color we associate with spirituality, wisdom, and power. Therefore, purple is a good choice to use in your Wisdom/Knowledge Gua to strengthen your connection with the higher worlds.

Choose plants with round or curved leaves for your living room. Plants with rounded leaves can encourage cooperation and unity among loved ones. You can fine-tune your results by selecting plants whose leaves and flowers define your intentions and by placing them in a specific gua. For example, I have a plant with heart-shaped leaves in the Relationships Gua of my living room. In the Helpful People/Travel Gua, I put a philodendron, which has leaves that curve at one end and are pointed at the other, symbolically blending congeniality with directness and mental stimulation.

Don't let magazines and newspapers clutter up your living room. Clutter in your living room symbolizes confusion in relationships with friends or family members. Magazines and newspapers are prime sources of clutter—as soon as you've read them, recycle them or pass them along. If you're in a hurry and don't have time to clean up paper clutter, at least straighten the piles of magazines and newspapers so they look neat.

Use thick rugs to promote a sense of security.

Thick, plushy, or nubby fabrics represent the earth element, whose qualities are security, warmth, and comfort. To emphasize these features in your social or family life, choose thick rugs that symbolize a sound, stable foundation underfoot.

TIP: Use rugs in earth colors to enhance further the qualities of security, warmth, and comfort.

Promote comfortable feelings with wooly-textured fabrics.

Wooly or nubby-textured fabrics invoke the earth element and promote feelings of security, connectedness, and comfort in your home. To encourage a sense of stability and nurturing among family members, choose upholstery covered with thick, plushy fabrics, preferably in earth tones.

Use fabric patterned with wavy lines in your Family/Community Gua.

Wavy lines are linked with flexibility and receptivity. To promote cooperation among family members and neighbors, use fabrics or wall coverings patterned with wavy lines or shapes (such as flowers, vines, swirls, spirals, or ripples) in the Family/Community Gua of your living room.

Use glass-topped coffee and end tables to spark lively conversations.

In China, glass is considered a "water" material, whose qualities include flexibility, versatility, and facile communication. If you seek intellectual companions and stimulating conversations with friends and housemates, place glass-topped tables and glass accessories in your living room.

Keep closet doors closed.

Closets represent private areas of your life. If your living room has a closet, make sure you keep the door closed so guests aren't privy to your "secrets."

Place an aquarium in your living room for good luck.

In feng shui, all living things are considered lucky, because they connect us with the Tao. Aquariums—especially when filled with goldfish (koi)—are thought to be particularly fortunate. (Notice how many Chinese restaurants feature aquariums in their décor.) To improve relationships with friends and family members, place a fish tank in your living room. If you also want to boost your prosperity, situate it in the Wealth Gua of your living room. If your goal is to attract contacts who can help you socially or financially, place the aquarium in your living room's Helpful People/Travel Gua.

Display the yin/yang symbol in the Relationships Gua.

This symbol represents the union of yin (feminine) and yang (masculine) energies to promote harmony. Display it in your living room's Relationships Gua to encourage peace and happiness between partners. (See page 23 for a picture of the yin/yang symbol.)

Install a ceiling fan to keep chi from getting stuck.

Chi can stagnate in a room when the windows are closed and no fresh air flows into your home. When chi can't circulate properly through your living room, you may experience stubbornness, poor communication, or bad feelings with household members or friends. To break up "stuck" chi, install a ceiling fan in your living room and let it keep air moving smoothly through your environment.

Repair or replace damaged furnishings.

Damaged, worn, or broken furnishings symbolize breaks, disappointments, or damaged relationships with friends or household members. In some cases, they can even lead to health problems. Repair or replace damaged items as soon as possible.

Replace burned-out lightbulbs.

As mentioned in Chapter 2, light augments chi and encourages clarity, optimism, and good feelings. To improve your social life, as well as relationships among family members, be sure to replace lightbulbs as soon as they burn out.

TIP: Use three-way bulbs or install dimmer switches on lamps so you can adjust light levels as necessary—bright lights stimulate chi and activity, while lower lighting promotes serenity.

Clear clutter in your Family/Community Gua.

To improve relationships with neighbors, relatives, and members of your community, clean up clutter in the Family/Community Gua of your living room. This cure is a good one to use if you are experiencing difficulties with neighbors or relatives who don't live with you.

Chapter 6

Coming Together to Eat: The Dining Room

Choose a round table to facilitate congeniality and unity.
Because circles symbolize unity and cooperation, eating together at a round dining table can help increase congeniality among household members. Think of the term "roundtable discussion," which suggests give-and-take. Unlike a rectangular table, which has a head and a foot, a round table doesn't contain hierarchical symbolism.

Choose a rectangular table to encourage expansion.

If your goal is to stimulate growth in any of the areas associated with the dining room (see Chapter 2, Looking Inside, page 29), a rectangular table is a better choice.

Choose an oval table to promote easy growth.

An oval combines the properties of a circle and a rectangle. If you wish to encourage growth in an area of your family or social life, or you'd like to improve your health or financial situation, an oval table can help you achieve your aims more gradually and gently than a rectangle will.

Choose a square table to ensure stability and security.

Squares offer stability. If you're trying to create a more secure, permanent home situation or want to stabilize your finances, health, or social structure, choose a square dining table.

Use a glass-topped dining table to spark pleasant conversation.

In feng shui, glass is linked with the water element, whose beneficial qualities include cooperation, receptivity, and communication. If your goal is to enjoy pleasant intellectual exchanges at dinner, furnish your dining room with a glass-topped table.

Choose a wooden table to promote growth.

As with rectangular objects, furniture made from wood encourages expansion. Choose a wooden table for your dining room if you'd like your family or your social circle to grow.

Position the table so the breadwinner's chair faces the dining room's entrance.

This cure helps improve the breadwinner's financial prospects. Seat this person so that she or he can clearly see the entrance to the dining room. In China, it's a sign of respect to give this seat to an honored guest.

Hang a picture that symbolizes togetherness in the Family/Community Gua.

This cure encourages positive feelings among household members, relatives, and neighbors. In your dining room's Family/Community Gua, hang a picture that shows people enjoying each other's company—a scene of a party, picnic, holiday gathering, vacation, or celebration, for example. Or display family photos here.

Place a round or oval rug under your table.

A round or oval rug encourages cooperation, unity, and a sense of togetherness. Place one under your dining table to promote harmonious feelings among household members.

TIP: Combine an oval or round rug with a rectangular or square table to attract the benefits of both.

Place a rectangular area rug under your table.

A rectangular rug in your dining room will spur growth. If you'd like to increase your family's size or expand your social circle, use a rectangular rug—especially one that includes green or blue in its design—under your table.

Paint your dining room walls yellow.

Yellow reminds us of the sun's rays and thus inspires warm, congenial feelings among diners. Because yellow complements most foods, it's a good choice for your dining room walls.

Don't paint your dining room white or gray.

In feng shui, white and gray correspond to the metal element and can produce stubbornness or rigidity among household members. White is also the color of mourning in China—not positive symbolism for dining.

Paint your dining room walls peach.

Peach combines the qualities of yellow, red, and white to bring good luck, optimism, and stability in areas associated with the dining room (see Chapter 2, Looking Inside, page 29). Because peach is a mildly stimulating color, it piques the appetite and is an ideal choice for your dining room. In China, peach is considered a fortunate color for people seeking love and romance.

Use green in your dining room's décor.

Green offers many positive associations, making it an ideal color for a dining room. It complements most foods and reminds us of leafy vegetables, thus promoting good health. A soothing yin color, it encourages diners to feel serene and facilitates digestion. Green is also a "wood" color and can therefore help increase your finances, family size, or social contacts.

Include red in your dining room's color scheme.

This lucky color should be included some place in your dining room—even if it's only a vase of red flowers on the table. Some people may find red too stimulating to use in large doses, but red walls in a dining room can give a sense of elegance in some decorating schemes.

Eat with chopsticks.

Wooden chopsticks encourage growth, as do all wooden objects. Eating with chopsticks also taps the symbolism of the number two, which can have a positive influence on partnerships.

Position six chairs around the table to encourage give-and-take.

Six is the number of give-and-take. To promote positive interpersonal exchange, cooperation, and sharing among household members, place six chairs around your dining room table.

Use red place mats for good luck.

To double your possibilities for good fortune, especially in money matters, use red place mats underneath your black dishes.

Combine warm and cool colors to create balance.

A combination of warm and cool colors in your dining room balances yin and yang to produce harmonious feelings among diners. Choose complementary hues for best results: Use pink or red with green; peach or orange with blue; or yellow with purple.

Combine all five elements in your dining room to establish balance.

To create a sense of balance and harmony, include all five elements in your dining room. For example, use a glass-topped (water) table with a metal base (metal), select four (earth) chairs, and place a rectangular (wood) Oriental rug that has red or orange (fire) in its design underneath the table.

Always keep a vase of fresh flowers on your dining room table.

Feng shui has ties to the Chinese nature religion Taoism. Place a vase of fresh flowers on your dining room table to connect diners with nature and to inspire positive feelings. As soon as the flowers start to wilt, remove them to avoid unwanted symbols of death and decay.

> **TIP: Choose flowers in colors that support your intentions. (See page 49 in Chapter 3, Fix Your Home, Fix Your Life, for more information about colors and their meanings.)**

Place two candles in silver or brass candleholders.

To strengthen or solidify a romantic relationship, put two candles in silver or brass candleholders on your dining room table. Two is the number of partnership; the metal element provides structure and permanence.

Put an I Ching coin under each diner's plate.

I Ching coins can be lucky talismans. Place one under each diner's plate to help bring him or her good fortune.

Give each diner his or her own candle.

Rather than using a candelabra or pair of candlesticks on your dining table, set a small votive candle at each person's place. This pretty "fire" cure attracts positive chi to each individual seated at the table.

Use images of horses to improve your health.

In China, horses represent longevity. In the West, we associate horses with power, freedom, and vitality. Tap into this positive symbolism by displaying a picture or sculpture of a horse in your dining room. The Health Gua is the best spot.

Mist your dining room with a fresh scent.

To clear the air and promote mental clarity, mist your dining room with a fresh, clean scent that's mildly stimulating. Citrus and mint are good choices.

Position four chairs around the table to increase stability.

The number four is linked with security and permanence. To help stabilize your finances, family relationships, or social contacts, place four chairs around your dining table.

Turn off the TV while eating.

TV can be a disruptive influence at mealtime. Watching programs that feature violence (such as the evening news) can upset digestion or exacerbate conflict between diners. Even upbeat shows distract diners from each other and interfere with the social aspects of sharing a meal.

Position two chairs at the table for romance.

The number two symbolizes partnership, so if your goal is to inspire romance, place two chairs at your dining table.

TIP: To encourage closeness and cooperation in a relationship, put one chair at the head of the table and one at the side, rather than one at the head and one at the foot, which places a symbolic barrier between the two individuals.

Ring a bell or gong before dinner.

The custom of ringing a gong or bell is more than just a way to call household members to dinner. This pleasing sound cure breaks up "stuck" chi and clears the air of unwanted vibrations that might interfere with healthy digestion.

Put a live plant in your dining room's Wealth Gua.

Because the dining room has connections with money, you can improve your finances by placing a healthy, live plant in the Wealth Gua of this room. Each time you water or trim the plant, you reinforce your intention to attract prosperity.

Create elemental balance on your dining table.

To establish harmony and balance, combine all five elements on your dining table. Here's an example: set the table with ceramic dishes (earth), chopsticks (wood), crystal or glassware (water), and candles (fire) in brass holders (metal). Use your imagination. (Refer to the Elemental Table on page 26 in Chapter 3, Fix Your Home, Fix Your Life.)

Keep clutter from piling up on your dining table.

If you don't eat in the dining room on a regular basis, the table may become a dumping zone. Clutter in the dining room can lead to confusion or upsets among household members or with social contacts. Keep your table free of clutter at all times, whether you eat in the dining room or not.

Avoid using your dining table as a desk or workstation.

Often the dining room ends up doing double duty as a workstation. Because work is incompatible with the social aspects of dining, try to avoid turning your dining table into a desk. If you don't have another option, at least clear the table of work-related materials before eating, and keep the area neat and clutter-free.

Use triangles to stimulate change.

This geometric shape corresponds to the fire element and suggests movement or change. Because a triangle has three points, it is also linked with the number three, which the Chinese consider auspicious. Display a triangular-shaped object in your dining room or use fabric with triangles, flame-shaped designs, or zigzags to spark change. Place the triangles in the gua that relates to the area of your life in which you desire change.

TIP: Don't position a triangle so it points directly at diners, as this produces what's known in feng shui as a "poison arrow" that can make people feel uncomfortable.

Serve food on black dishes.

In China, black is considered a fortunate color where money is concerned. Eating from black dishes can inspire financial good luck.

Chapter 7

The Heart of the Home: The Kitchen

Hang a mirror above the stove.

In feng shui, the stove is considered a source of good luck and prosperity. Because mirrors visually "double" the power of whatever objects they reflect, hanging one above your stove symbolically doubles its power to bring you good fortune. A mirror serves another purpose here, too. When the cook is preparing food, he or she may not be able to see people entering the kitchen. The mirror allows the cook to see behind him or her without turning around.

TIP: An octagon-shaped bagua mirror is best.

Keep your stove clean and in good working order.

A stove can only generate good luck if it is functioning properly. A damaged or dirty stove will produce the opposite effect. In feng shui, the stove is also connected with health—here is where the cook prepares food to nourish the household members. Make sure your stove is clean and in optimal condition so you can attract health and wealth into your home.

Use your stove every day.

If you don't use your stove regularly, you'll limit your good fortune. Turn on the stove and boil water every day, even if you don't actually cook anything.

Don't store knives in the kitchen's Relationships Gua.

Knives can symbolize sharp words or cutting ties. If placed in the Relationships Gua, they may have a destructive effect on a primary partnership. Move them to another location.

Use green in your decorating scheme to promote good health.

From both a symbolic and a practical perspective, feng shui links the kitchen with health. Green is the color of vegetables and plants, so this color has positive associations with nutrition. When you include green in your kitchen's color scheme—especially in the Health Gua—you demonstrate your desire for good health and invite well-being into your home.

Mist your kitchen with citrus scent.

The fresh, clean scent of citrus can clear the air in your kitchen—literally and figuratively. Lemon, lime, orange, and grapefruit aromas also stimulate the mind and refresh your spirit. Pour a few drops of essential oil into a bottle of water and mist your kitchen with the mixture periodically.

Use gold in your decorating scheme to attract wealth.

Because feng shui connects the kitchen with wealth, you can increase your money-drawing power by using the color gold in your kitchen. Bright golden tones also remind us of the sun's life-giving energy and therefore increase optimism. Paint your kitchen walls a sunny yellow-gold to boost prosperity and happiness.

Use orange to stimulate appetite.

Studies show that fiery colors, particularly orange, tend to stimulate appetite, so this is an ideal hue to use in the kitchen. If bright orange is too strong for your taste, try peach, apricot, or terra-cotta instead. Or incorporate a few flame-orange accents into your kitchen's décor.

Keep the kitchen's Health Gua free of clutter.

The center of your kitchen is the Health Gua. Because clutter represents blockages, stress, and confusion, it can lead to health problems if you allow it to accumulate in the middle of your kitchen. Keep this area free and clear to encourage good health in family members.

Use a square kitchen table to increase stability.

Squares symbolize stability and permanence. To encourage a sense of security and structure in your family, use a square table in your kitchen.

Keep passageways through your kitchen free of clutter and obstacles.
From a practical standpoint, cluttered walkways in your kitchen might pose health or safety risks. From the perspective of feng shui, clutter obstructs the smooth flow of chi, thereby hampering the flow of health and wealth into your life. Clear the traffic patterns through your kitchen to enhance your physical and financial well-being.

Choose black appliances to encourage prosperity.
In China, black is considered the color of wealth. Therefore, it's a good color to include in your kitchen. Black appliances—especially the stove, which generates wealth—can help you attract prosperity. (As mentioned earlier, make sure your stove is in good working order for best results.)

Choose white appliances to promote stability in your home.

The Chinese connect white with the metal element, which provides stability and structure. To enhance your family's sense of order, permanence, and structure, choose white appliances for your kitchen.

Tie a red ribbon around your faucet for good luck.

This cure helps keep chi from slipping away down the drain. Red is considered a lucky color in China so to attract good fortune into your home, tie a red ribbon around your kitchen faucet. Each time you turn on the tap, you'll be reminded of your goal to increase your luck.

Set up a shrine in your kitchen's Wisdom/Knowledge Gua.

This may sound strange to Westerners, but the Chinese often create shrines to the Kitchen God to attract blessings. Place symbols of your faith in the Wisdom/Knowledge Gua of your kitchen to invite the Three Great Blessings—health, wealth, and happiness—into your home.

Allow space on either side of your stove.

The stove generates wealth, but if it is crammed into a corner of your kitchen, its money-drawing power will be limited. If possible, position your stove so there's plenty of counter space on either side of it. If this isn't possible, hang a small mirror on the enclosed side to open up the area symbolically.

Put the telephone in the Family/Community Gua.

To facilitate good communication among family members, neighbors, and others in your community, place the telephone in the Family/Community Gua of your kitchen.

TIP: A black phone is best because black, a "water" color, emphasizes clear communication and fortunate contacts.

Store pots and pans in the kitchen's Wealth Gua.

Metal objects symbolize structure and permanence. If you wish to keep your finances stable and secure, store pots and pans in the Wealth Gua of your kitchen.

Prevent clutter from piling up on your countertops.

Not only is clutter unsightly, but it can also pose health and safety hazards when it accumulates on your kitchen countertops. Clutter also represents confusion, stress, and obstacles— which, in your kitchen, can translate into health or money problems. Keep your countertops free of clutter for practical reasons as well as symbolic ones.

Use a round kitchen table to encourage family harmony.

The circle is a universal symbol of unity. To promote harmony and cooperation among family members, put a round table in your kitchen and eat there together often.

Make sure your kitchen door opens easily.

In many homes, the kitchen door is the one most frequently used. Therefore, this is where chi enters your living space. If the door sticks or can't be opened completely, chi will have a hard time getting inside to energize your home. Adjust the door so it opens and closes easily, and clear away any obstructions that block it.

Keep kitchen cabinets, drawers, and closets neat and orderly.

Closets symbolize the secret or unseen parts of our lives. In the kitchen, cabinets and closets represent the hidden factors that can influence your health and wealth. Keep these storage areas neat and orderly to avoid complications, blockages, or confusion regarding your physical or financial well-being. Go through cabinets and closets regularly and get rid of food whose shelf life has expired or of objects you no longer use.

Put round knobs on kitchen cabinets.

Kitchens tend to have lots of straight lines and sharp angles in them, which can provoke stress. Offset this by putting round knobs on cabinet doors and drawers.

Clean out your refrigerator regularly.

Make a point of cleaning out your refrigerator weekly. Not only is spoiled food a health risk, but it also symbolizes waste and old, unwanted stuff that no longer has a place in your life. Clear clutter from your fridge to rid your kitchen of these unpleasant associations.

Use a glass-topped table to facilitate communication.

In the Chinese elemental system, glass belongs to the water category, whose qualities include flexibility and receptivity. To encourage easy, open communication among family members, use a kitchen table with a glass top.

Combine all five Chinese elements in your kitchen.

Feng shui is all about balance, and one way to achieve balance in your kitchen is to combine all five of the Chinese elements: earth, water, wood, fire, and metal. (See Chapter 3, Fix Your Home, Fix Your Life, on page 49 for more information.) Most kitchens feature wooden cabinets, metal appliances, and plumbing (water). The stove represents the fire element, but earth may be lacking unless you include something made of ceramic or stone. If possible, opt for a tile floor or granite counter-tops. If that's not an option, use pottery or stone accessories to incorporate the earth element into your kitchen.

Position the microwave in your kitchen's Wealth Gua.

If you can't place your stove in the Wealth Gua of your kitchen, position the microwave there to promote prosperity. (Note: Some feng shui practitioners believe you should not put the microwave above the stove because anything heavy will depress the chi that is generated by the stove and thus limit your wealth.)

Clean kitchen windows to promote good health.

In feng shui, windows symbolize the eyes. Dirty windows cloud your ability to see clearly and may cause confusion about health matters. Washing your kitchen windows can help you see your way to better health and well-being.

Position the stove in the Wealth Gua of your kitchen.

The best place to locate your stove is in the Wealth Gua of your kitchen. The Chinese believe the stove generates prosperity, so positioning it in the Wealth Gua increases its power and, thus, your ability to attract good fortune.

Put something red in your kitchen for good luck.

In China, red is considered lucky. To attract good fortune to your home, include red in your kitchen's decorating scheme. Choose the gua in which you most desire luck.

Hang a plant above your sink to prevent financial losses.

The drains in your home literally drain chi from your environment. To keep money from going "down the drain," hang a plant above your sink. Plants, which symbolize life and growth, serve to offset the devitalizing quality of the drain.

TIP: Plants with red or purple flowers are best.

Place a vase of fresh flowers in your kitchen's Family/Community Gua.

Flowers symbolize love and life, so they can help promote positive feelings among family members. Set a vase of fresh flowers on your kitchen table for loved ones to enjoy. Remove flowers as soon as they start to wilt and replace them with fresh ones.

Display family photographs in the Family/Community Gua.
Instead of displaying family photos on the refrigerator, frame them and hang them in the Family/Community Gua of your kitchen. Pictures that depict household members having fun together will encourage positive feelings and strengthen bonds among loved ones.

Choose a ceramic tile floor to promote security.
Ceramic tile falls into the earth category in the Chinese elemental system. This element encourages feelings of security and comfort, so choosing a ceramic tile floor for your kitchen helps promote these qualities in your domestic life. It can also help secure your financial assets.

Chapter 8

Rest and Romance: The Master Bedroom

Position the bed so you can see the door.

If you can see the entrance to your bedroom when you are in bed, you'll feel secure and comfortable—no one can enter without your knowledge. Place the bed so that it faces the door, preferably in a spot that is as far away from the doorway as possible (putting the bed in the Relationships Gua is ideal).

Don't place the bed near the door.

If your bed is too close to the door, your rest may be disturbed by noises outside. You might also feel uncomfortable because you don't have enough privacy. Position the bed so that it isn't easily visible or in direct line with the room's entrance.

Don't put your bed under a slanted ceiling.

A slanted ceiling or eaves reduce the amount of chi that can circulate around your bed. Some people even experience physical complaints or have trouble sleeping when their beds are positioned beneath a sloped ceiling. Move your bed to a more favorable spot.

Don't put your bed under a beam.

A heavy beam above your bed can also depress chi and lead to physical problems. Reposition your bed so it isn't directly beneath a beam.

Avoid "poison arrows" in your bedroom.

In feng shui, sharp angles and corners that point at you when you are sitting or lying down are called "poison arrows." These angles cause subconscious stress. To prevent restlessness, arrange chests of drawers and other pieces of furniture so that their corners don't point directly at you when you are in bed.

Keep closet doors shut.

To avoid being distracted by the energies of the things in your closet, keep closet doors closed.

Place matching nightstands on either side of the bed.

The number two signifies partnership and harmony. To encourage feelings of togetherness and cooperation, place matching nightstands on both sides of your bed.

Place matching lamps on either side of the bed.

Light is a favorite activating and augmenting feng shui cure. To increase the positive energy in a primary partnership or to brighten your romantic prospects, place a pair of matching lamps in your master bedroom, one on either side of the bed.

Place a light in the Relationships Gua of your bedroom.

To light up your love life, place a lamp in the Relationships Gua. This cure brings the fire element into this gua and focuses chi on this part of your life.

Position a large piece of furniture in the Relationships Gua.

Another way to stabilize a relationship is to place a large piece of furniture in the Relationships Gua of your master bedroom. Heavy objects help hold down things that might otherwise slip away.

Use pink in your decorating scheme to encourage loving feelings.

Pink is associated with romance, affection, and joy. Use pink in your master bedroom to attract love and happiness in a primary partnership.

> **TIP: The best place to use pink is in the bedroom's Relationships Gua.**

Use red in your decorating scheme to spark passion.

We connect red with passion and vitality, so it's a good color to use in your master bedroom if you want to turn up the heat in a romantic relationship. Because red is a stimulating color, it may be too strong to use in large doses—it could interfere with restful sleep. Place something red in your bedroom's Relationships Gua—red flowers, a big red heart, red throw pillows, or a picture in a red frame.

Paint your bedroom peach to attract new love.

In China, the color peach is believed to attract romance—the term "peach blossom luck" refers to someone who is lucky in love. If you want to begin a new relationship, paint your bedroom peach.

Tie a nine-inch-long red ribbon on your bedroom's doorknob.

This cure combines two lucky symbols: the color red and the number nine. Tie the ribbon on the doorknob of your master bedroom to attract good luck and to invite love into your life.

Paint bedroom walls white to strengthen commitment.

White, a "metal" color, is linked with permanence and structure. To strengthen the commitment and stability in a romantic relationship, paint the walls in your master bedroom white.

Use blue in your decorating scheme to promote tranquility.

Blue's soothing qualities promote feelings of tranquility and help you relax. Paint your bedroom walls blue to let you unwind at the end of the day and sleep better. Or use blue linens on your bed.

Put something purple in your Wisdom/Knowledge Gua to encourage meaningful dreams.

Purple is the color of the crown chakra, the energy center at the top of your head through which you receive higher knowledge. If you want to gain insights and guidance while you sleep, place something purple in the Wisdom/Knowledge Gua of your bedroom. This cure can also inspire meaningful or vivid dreams.

Place spiritual objects or images in your Wisdom/Knowledge Gua.
To strengthen your connection with a higher power, place objects that represent your faith in the Wisdom/Knowledge Gua of your bedroom. These symbols can also help you relax and sleep better by promoting feelings of security, trust, and serenity.

TIP: From the perspective of feng shui, a statue of Kwan Yin or the Buddha would be the ideal object to put in your Wisdom/Knowledge Gua, regardless of your religious beliefs.

Hang a pleasing image on the ceiling above your bed.
Make sure the first thing you see each morning is something happy. To start your day off on the right foot, hang an attractive picture or other positive symbol on the ceiling above your bed.

Place a piece of rose quartz on the nightstand.

Rose quartz emits gentle, pleasing vibrations that can promote harmony and ease in a relationship. As a result, this semiprecious gemstone is often associated with love and affection. Place a smooth, tumbled chunk of rose quartz on your nightstand to encourage happiness in a romantic partnership.

Place two candles in your bedroom to promote togetherness.

This cure combines two symbolic feng shui cures: the fire element and the number two. Fire stimulates enthusiasm and passion, and the number two represents partnership and togetherness. Candlelight, as we all know, invites romance.

> **TIP: Choose red or pink candles, depending on how much excitement you desire.**

Put a circular object in your Relationships Gua.

Circles are universal symbols of unity and wholeness. To improve harmony and cooperation in a relationship, place a circular object in the Relationships Gua of the master bedroom—a mirror, lamp, clock, table, or vase, for instance.

Don't let dirty laundry collect in your bedroom.

Chi gets stuck on dirt, resulting in stagnant conditions. "Dirty laundry" also represents unpleasant business and secrets which can damage a romantic partnership. Instead of using a clothes hamper in your master bedroom, put dirty clothes in a hall closet, bathroom, or other area of your home.

Keep your bedroom free of clutter.

Clutter represents confusion, upsets, and old attitudes or behaviors that can cause problems in a primary partnership. Clear clutter from your master bedroom to promote clarity and comfort in your love life.

Clean out your bedroom closet regularly.

Old clothes you no longer wear and other outdated articles symbolize the past. To keep your love life fresh and lively, clean out your bedroom closet at least twice a year and get rid of things you no longer use or that have negative associations for you.

Replace a faded bedspread or drapes.

Faded fabrics suggest that a relationship has lost its color. Revitalize a romantic partnership by replacing an old, faded bedspread or drapes with something bright and new.

Don't store anything under the bed.

When you store things under your bed, you prevent chi from moving freely through the area. As a result, you may not sleep well or your vitality may be compromised. If storage space is precious and you must place things under the bed, make sure what you put there has positive, restful associations for you.

Remove objects with disruptive associations from your bedroom.

All objects generate energy-make sure everything in your bedroom represents peace, love, and contentment. I used to know a man who kept his gun collection in a safe in his bedroom, which generated subconscious feelings of violence and fear instead of relaxation and romance. Another had a stuffed deer head above the bed until his wife made him remove it and hang it in the garage.

Wash the windows in your bedroom.

In feng shui, windows represent the eyes. To see a relationship or a situation with a partner more clearly, wash the windows in your master bedroom.

Place a vase of red or pink roses in your bedroom.

We associate roses with love and romance, but in feng shui they also represent growth. Put fresh flowers in your master bedroom to express your love—red and pink are good choices because these colors are linked with affection and passion.

Burn rose, jasmine, musk, or ylang-ylang incense to spark romance.

These sensual scents stimulate loving feelings. Burning incense also brings the fire element into your bedroom and helps ignite romance.

Burn lavender incense to promote relaxation.

Lavender's soothing scent helps reduce stress and anxiety. Burn lavender incense at the end of the day to help you relax and sleep better.

Hang two bells on a doorknob.

Tie two bells on the doorknob of your master bedroom to encourage romantic harmony. Before entering your bedroom, ring the bells to disperse any stuck or negative chi that might be lingering in the room.

Don't put a computer or TV in your bedroom.

Computers and TVs are incompatible with romance and can take your attention away from your partner. Don't put them in your master bedroom.

Play a singing bowl in your bedroom.

Singing bowls emit wonderful, pure tones that can clear unwanted energies from your bedroom and fill the space with desired vibrations. Often these bowls are tuned to play a particular note that corresponds to one of the body's chakras or vital energy centers. Choose a bowl that is designed to harmonize with the heart or sacral chakra to enhance romance, or with the brow or crown chakra to facilitate peaceful sleep and meaningful dreams.

Place a healthy plant with rounded leaves in your bedroom.

On a symbolic level, plants signify growth and life. On a practical level, they absorb carbon dioxide from the air. Put a live plant in your bedroom to promote good health and restful sleep. Because circles represent comfort, cooperation, and unity, a plant with rounded leaves can help foster positive feelings with a romantic partner.

Remove sharp objects from your Relationships Gua.

Sharp objects can signify sharp words or hurtful actions. Remove any sharp items from the Relationships Gua of your master bedroom to help keep your love life functioning pleasantly.

Mist bed linens with a romantic or sensual fragrance.

To inspire loving feelings, mist your bed linens with ylang-ylang, rose, musk, jasmine, or another sensual fragrance.

Store linens with potpourri or a sensual-scented sachet.

Like the previous cure, this one uses the subtle power of aromatherapy to spark romance. After washing your bed linens, store them in a drawer with a sachet or potpourri that includes romantic scents such as ylang-ylang, rose, musk, or jasmine.

Hang pictures that symbolize love in your Relationships Gua.

This cure taps into the power of symbols to enhance romantic feelings. Hang a picture of a happy couple, a heart, roses, or another image that says "love" to you in the Relationships Gua of your master bedroom. This is the perfect spot to display wedding photos or pictures of you and your partner.

TIP: Use a wooden frame if you want your love to grow and a metal one if your goal is to strengthen or stabilize your relationship.

Hang pictures in your bedroom that convey a sense of rest and relaxation.

To encourage rest and relaxation, hang pictures of peaceful landscapes or other soothing images in your bedroom.

Decorate with wooden furniture to encourage growth.

Wooden furniture inspires expansion, so if your goal is to attract a romantic partner or increase the passion in an existing relationship, use wooden pieces in your master bedroom.

TIP: This cure is also good for couples who want to have a baby.

Use a brass or metal bed to increase stability in a relationship.

A brass or wrought-iron bed uses the energies of the metal element to strengthen the bond between romantic partners and increase the commitment in a relationship.

Choose fabrics with curved, round, or wavy patterns for your bedroom.

To improve congeniality, cooperation, and receptivity in a romantic partnership, decorate your master bedroom with fabrics that feature rounded or wavy patterns.

Use a round or oval area rug in your bedroom.

Most bedroom furniture is rectangular in shape. Curves promote relaxation, while sharp angles and straight lines produce stress. To offset a preponderance of angles and straight lines in your bedroom, put a round or oval area rug on the floor.

Put round knobs on dresser drawers.

Here's another way to incorporate circles into your bedroom—replace square or rectangular pulls on dresser drawers with round knobs.

Use an image of doves to enhance your love.

Doves are popular symbols of love and partnership. Place a picture of two doves in your Relationships Gua to enhance loving feelings.

Put an image of a crane in your Creativity/Children Gua.

Couples who want to have a baby can display a picture of a crane in the Creativity/Children Gua of the master bedroom. The crane is considered fortunate in China and symbolizes fertility in many parts of the world.

Avoid triangles in your bedroom.

Triangles are the most stimulating of all shapes. Flame patterns, mountains, pyramids, some lampshades, and plants with pointed leaves all form triangles. To prevent the stress and restlessness that triangles can produce, eliminate them from your bedroom.

Use a wind chime to soothe tension.

To disperse "stuck" chi or negative vibrations, hang a wind chime in your bedroom window. The pleasing sound also has a soothing effect and can help you relax at the end of the day.

Hang a wind chime in a window facing noisy neighbors.

This motion cure helps deflect the disruptive energies caused by noisy or unpleasant neighbors. Hang a wind chime in a bedroom window that faces the neighboring building.

Place a fan in your bedroom window.

Like the previous cures, this one uses motion to disperse and deflect unwanted energies away from your master bedroom. Because fans activate chi, this cure can also help stimulate your love life.

Chapter 9

Bedtime Stories: Children's Bedrooms

Place books in the Wisdom/Knowledge Gua of a child's room.

To encourage learning and help your child improve his or her grades, place books and other study materials in the Wisdom/Knowledge Gua.

Put a child's desk and computer in the Wisdom/Knowledge Gua.

Positioning a child's desk and computer in the Wisdom/Knowledge Gua of his room will have a similar effect as the previous cure. If your child primarily plays video games on the computer, however, move it to another part of the room.

Position the bed so that when the child is in it, she can see the room's entrance.

Position children's beds so that when they are in bed, they can easily view the door to the room. This placement provides comfort and security, because it allows children to see immediately anyone who enters their rooms.

Don't place a child's bed under eaves or a slanted ceiling.

A slanted ceiling can depress chi and interfere with the optimal flow of life-giving energy. Some people complain of headaches or respiratory problems caused by sleeping under an angled ceiling. Don't position a child's bed under a slant—you may limit the amount of chi that's available to him or her.

Hang a mirror or picture on a slanted ceiling.

If space is limited and you can't avoid placing the bed under a slanted ceiling, hang a small mirror above the bed to open up the space symbolically. This cure alleviates the pressure and constriction caused by a low ceiling. A picture of a peaceful landscape with a distant view can create the same sense of openness and relief.

Avoid using a lot of red or orange in a child's room.

Red and orange are stimulating colors and may be too stressful to use in children's bedrooms. Vibrant, fiery colors can interfere with a child's sleep or concentration. In large doses, they may also promote assertiveness or tension that can lead to problems with siblings or friends. Because red is considered lucky, however, it's a good accent color.

Paint bedroom walls white to improve concentration.

Does your child have trouble focusing or completing tasks? Paint the walls in his or her bedroom white to improve concentration and persistence.

Paint bedroom walls yellow to inspire creativity.

Yellow reminds us of the sun's light and promotes feelings of warmth, optimism, and enthusiasm. It's also a good color for artists and other creative people. To encourage your child's imagination, paint his or her bedroom walls yellow.

Use green in the color scheme to encourage serenity.

Green has a calming, stabilizing effect on us. Because we associate green with nature and plants, it can also make us feel secure and grounded. To help a nervous, anxious, or very active child feel more calm and centered, paint his or her bedroom walls green.

Put something pink in the Helpful People/Travel Gua.

Often we avoid using pink in boys' bedrooms, but this color may be more beneficial (and necessary) for them than for girls. Pink encourages cooperation and congenial feelings. Emphasizing this color in the Helpful People/Travel Gua of the child's bedroom can improve relationships with companions. It also helps a shy child make friends. A ruffled pink bedspread might not be appropriate, but how about artwork or a plant with pink flowers?

Put something pink in the Self/Identity Gua.

Many children and teens experience concerns regarding their sense of self or identity. To help them overcome this, place something pink in the Self/Identity Gua of their bedrooms. Pink—especially fuchsia or hot pink—is the color of self-love, so it can improve an insecure child's confidence and self-esteem.

Place something purple in the Self/Identity Gua.

In China, purple is considered even luckier than red. It also implies power, spirituality, and authority. When you place something purple in a child's Self/Identity Gua, you help boost his or her personal power and good fortune.

Use a brown or tan rug to steady emotions and increase trust.

Brown, an earth color in both Eastern and Western traditions, can help a nervous or very sensitive child feel more safe and secure. Because a rug symbolizes one's footing, place a brown or tan rug in the child's bedroom to provide a stable foundation.

Decorate with metal furnishings to encourage structure and determination.

In the Chinese elemental system, metal is associated with strength, permanence, stability, and focus. Metal furniture, such as a brass bed or a metal desk, can improve a child's persistence and concentration. The metal element also provides a sense of stability and structure for children whose lives are in flux or who feel insecure. To prevent stasis, however, consider combining metal furnishings with some wooden pieces, which stimulate expansion.

Decorate with wood furnishings to encourage growth.

In the Chinese elemental system, wood is associated with expansion. Wood furniture helps stimulate healthy growth, mentally, physically, and emotionally. To modulate growth, however, combine wood furniture with metal pieces.

Use a round area rug to promote cooperation and harmony.

Because circles symbolize union and wholeness, they can encourage children to cooperate with others. Place a round area rug in a child's bedroom to promote feelings of peace, harmony, and togetherness. This is especially important if two or more children share the same bedroom or if sibling rivalry exists in your home. Try to position furniture so that each piece rests partly on the rug to create a sense of unity.

Include thick, plush fabrics to provide a sense of security and well-being.

Thick, soft, heavily textured fabrics—particularly those made of natural fibers—bring the earth element into a child's bedroom. Because the earth element enhances security and permanence, using plush rugs or nubby-textured bedspreads can be comforting to young children.

Choose blue bed linens to help a child sleep better.

Blue is a cool, restful color that we associate with peace and quiet. As discussed in Chapter 3, Fix Your Home, Fix Your Life (page 49), test subjects placed in blue rooms tend to feel calm and relaxed. To help a child sleep better, put blue linens on his or her bed.

TIP: Dark blue is better than cobalt or pale blue.

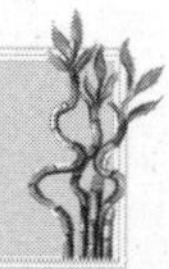

Mist a child's bed linens with lavender.

The scent of lavender calms the mind and encourages relaxation. Before putting children to bed, lightly mist their pillows with a mixture of pure essential oil of lavender diluted in water. The soothing fragrance will help them unwind and sleep better.

Use vanilla incense to produce feelings of comfort and contentment.

Vanilla is a calming scent and can help ease stress and anxiety. It also reminds many people of baking and sparks other nourishing memories. Burn vanilla-scented incense in a child's room to instill feelings of comfort and contentment.

Give a child a piece of amethyst.

Amethysts have long been associated with dreams. Their gentle vibrations also help soothe the mind and emotions. To help a child relax before bed, give him a large, tumbled amethyst to rub. An amethyst placed under a child's pillow or on the nightstand can prompt sweet dreams.

Hang a crystal in a child's bedroom window.

Crystals serve as prisms, breaking down sunlight into pretty rainbows. Hang a faceted crystal in the window of a child's bedroom to bring all the colors of the visible spectrum into his or her space. This cure helps produce wholeness and balance.

TIP: Choose a crystal whose shape symbolizes something positive. I have a crystal heart hanging in my bedroom window and a crystal bird in my office. Your child might like a unicorn or a star.

Don't place a TV in the Wisdom/Knowledge Gua.

The TV shouldn't be the main source of information for a child, but if you place a television in the Wisdom/Knowledge Gua of her bedroom, you encourage this tendency.

Don't place a TV in the Helpful People/Travel Gua.

The TV shouldn't serve as a companion for children. If a television is located in the Helpful People/travel Gua of a child's room, however, he or she may be less likely to socialize with friends and might turn to the TV for company instead.

Keep the center of a child's room free of clutter.

The center of the room corresponds to health. Clutter in this area can lead to health-related problems, so be sure to keep the space clear.

Install a pegboard at "kid height."

Make it easy for kids to hang up their clothes and keep their rooms neat. Install pegboards at a height that's convenient for them to reach.

TIP: Adjust clothing rods in children's closets to a convenient height, too.

Hang family photos in the Family/Community Gua.

To improve a child's relationships with family members, hang photographs of parents, siblings, and other relatives in the Family/Community Gua of her bedroom. Pictures of loved ones can also help a young or insecure child feel safe and connected. Make sure the photos show happy interactions among the people involved.

Hang photos of friends in the Helpful People/Travel Gua.

Displaying photographs of a child's friends in the Helpful People/Travel Gua can enhance relationships with playmates. If a child is having trouble making friends, hang magazine pictures or paintings of children playing together happily in this gua of your child's bedroom to help attract companions.

Display awards, trophies, and symbols of success in the Fame/Future Gua.

You can encourage a child's success by placing symbols of his or her accomplishments in the Fame/Future Gua. Each time the child views trophies, awards, ribbons, diplomas, and other signs of achievement, he or she will be prompted subconsciously to reach for the stars. Acknowledging triumphs also reinforces a child's sense of self-esteem.

Place images of a child's goals in the Fame/Future Gua.

What does your child want to be when he or she grows up? Let the child choose photos or other images that represent his or her future goals. Then display them prominently in the Fame/Future Gua of your child's room to keep those goals in the forefront of his or her mind.

Place three objects in the Fame/Future Gua of a child's room.

Three is a lucky number in feng shui. It also stimulates change and encourages action in a particular direction. If your children aren't performing up to their abilities, place three objects in the Fame/Future Gua of their bedrooms to inspire them to achieve greater heights. Make sure the objects you choose represent positive goals and success.

Train children to keep their rooms neat and orderly.

Clutter equates with confusion, lack of direction, and instability. Large-scale clutter can even create obstacles in a child's life. Studies show that children who keep their rooms orderly tend to do better in school and are more well-adjusted emotionally. Train kids to pick up after themselves and organize their belongings, not only for practical reasons, but to assist in their personal growth as well. (See my books *10-Minute Clutter Control* and *10-Minute Clutter Control Room by Room* for more information.)

Rearrange the furniture periodically.

Whenever you change something in your home, you stimulate change in your life. Because children change so quickly, it's a good idea to rearrange the furniture in their bedrooms periodically—say, every six months or so—to keep pace with their growth and inspire them to continue evolving. If a child is experiencing anxiety in connection with frequent or stressful life changes, however, you can help balance the upsets by leaving furniture in the same place for a longer period.

Store arts and crafts supplies in the Creativity/Children Gua.

To support and stimulate a child's creativity, store arts and crafts supplies in the Creativity/Children Gua of his bedroom. This is also a good spot for housing a child's hobbies or collections.

Provide open shelving for toys and games.

Open shelving provides an easy place for kids to put toys and games away when they're finished playing with them and helps keep clutter at bay.

Display children's drawings in the Creativity/Children Gua.

Children's drawings, models, and other creative projects should be displayed in the Creativity/Children Gua to encourage continued artistic growth. Rotate artwork regularly to stimulate a child's imagination.

Get rid of children's outgrown clothing promptly.

It's not unusual for parents to hold on to children's outgrown clothing. However, if you aren't keeping it for younger siblings, get rid of it rather than storing it. Hanging on to things from an earlier stage in the child's life can indicate that you may be reluctant to let the child grow up. Give old clothes to charity or take lightly used ones to a consignment shop so others can benefit from them.

Give away children's outgrown toys and games.

Get rid of toys and games that children have outgrown, too. Like the previous situation, holding on to these mementos of bygone days can keep you and your kids stuck in the past. Pass them on to younger neighbors or siblings, or let kids hold a yard sale to make extra cash.

Hang a round mirror in the Family/Community Gua of a teenager's room.

Circles are ancient symbols of unity and harmony. To encourage a teenager to spend more time with family members, or to be more coöperative and congenial, hang a round mirror in the Family/Community Gua of his bedroom.

Place six matching items in the Family/Community Gua.

Six is the number of give-and-take. To encourage sharing and cooperation among family members, group six matching or similar items in the Family/Community Gua of a child's bedroom. Make sure the objects symbolize congeniality, positive interaction, or teamwork.

Place a plant in the Wisdom/Knowledge Gua to improve a child's grades.

Plants represent growth. To help children improve their grades and stimulate their curiosity, put a healthy, live plant in the Wisdom/Knowledge Gua. Instruct them in the proper care of the plant. By watering, feeding, and trimming it regularly, they symbolically nurture their own intellectual growth.

Let children participate in decorating their rooms.

Often children intuitively know what they need. Feng shui works at a subconscious or feeling level, as well as at a practical one. Therefore, children may reveal their strengths, weaknesses, concerns, and hopes through their decorating choices. An insecure child may naturally gravitate toward furnishings that fall into the "earth" or "metal" category, for instance.

Pay attention to the areas where clutter collects.

Clutter represents confusion, upsets, obstacles, and stress. Notice which guas tend to become cluttered in a child's room—these indicate the parts of his or her life that are unsettled or causing problems. By clearing away the clutter and organizing their belongings, children can help bring order and clarity into their lives.

Chapter 10

Hospitality Suites: Guest Rooms

Position the bed(s) so occupants can see the entrance door easily. Make guests feel comfortable by positioning the bed(s) so occupants can see the door to the bedroom when they are in bed. This prevents someone from entering the room unseen and startling your guests. Try to place the bed as far away from the door as possible to afford more privacy and quiet.

Hang a mirror so that it reflects the guest room door.

If you can't situate the bed in the ideal place, hang a mirror on the wall so that when your guests are in bed, they can see the entrance to the room reflected in the mirror. This allows them to see anyone who might enter the room and avoid surprises.

Provide space in a guest room closet.

Guest room closets frequently serve as additional storage sites for family members' belongings. To make guests feel welcome, however, clear a space in the closet for them to hang their clothing. A full closet indicates that there's no room for anyone else in your home.

Use curved headboards to promote comfort.

Curves and circles are more restful than sharp lines and angles because they conduct chi in a gentle manner. To promote comfort and rest in your guest room, choose a curved headboard instead of an angular one.

Remove items that might interfere with a guest's comfort.

Guest rooms often serve multiple purposes—they may double as home offices, workout rooms, or storage areas. To ensure that your guests enjoy a comfortable, restful visit, remove items such as computers, exercise equipment, or hobby and craft supplies that might interfere with their comfort. If you can't relocate these items, consider covering or screening them from your guests' view.

Clear clutter from under the bed(s).

Clutter stored under the bed can interfere with the smooth flow of chi through your guest room. It may be tempting to use this space, especially in a small home or apartment, but be aware of what you store under the bed—make sure its nature and symbolic associations are compatible with rest and relaxation.

Use down comforters to make guests feel welcome.

Fluffy down comforters bring the earth element into your guest room. This element's characteristics include security, comfort, and stability, which will help make your guests feel welcome.

TIP: Work on improving your home's feng shui when you are at your energy peak. We all have peaks and valleys in our diurnal cycles. Designate a time to clear clutter and improve balance when your energy level is high. When you feel yourself getting tired or feel your enthusiasm wane, just stop. Schedule another day to pick up where you left off. Your goal should be to feel positive about what you're doing. Don't let yourself get overwhelmed.

Paint a guest room blue to encourage restful sleep.

Blue's soothing qualities help relieve stress at the end of the day and promote rest and relaxation. Paint the walls of your guest room blue to help guests sleep soundly.

Paint a guest room green to inspire serenity.

Green is another yin color that encourages restful feelings. Paint the walls of your guest room green to suggest the serenity of a peaceful forest or meadow.

Paint a guest room peach to attract happiness.

Peach blends the optimism of yellow with the affection and congeniality of pink. Paint your guest room peach to create a pleasing, cheerful mood for visitors.

Ring a bell before guests retire.

If your guest room is unoccupied much of the time, chi may stagnate there from lack of use or activity. Before your guests retire, ring a bell in the room to break up stuck chi and chase away any "bad vibes" that may linger there.

Place a vase of flowers in the Helpful People/Travel Gua.

This welcoming gesture lets guests know you are happy to have them in your home. It also encourages continued positive relationships with friends in the future. If your guests are relatives, put flowers in the Family/Community Gua instead.

Place four objects on the nightstand for an extended stay.

If you want your guests to stay for an extended period of time, place four objects on the nightstand in your guest room. Four is the number of stability and permanence, so it discourages change or movement.

Place five objects on the nightstand for a short visit.

If you don't want your guests to stick around long, place five objects on the nightstand in your guest room. Five is the number of change, so it sparks restlessness and a desire for movement.

Mist your guest room with a calming scent.

To help guests relax and feel comfortable in your home, mist their room with a soothing scent, such as vanilla or lavender. If a guest wears a particular scent, you may choose to spray this familiar fragrance in the room to make him or her feel at home.

Put the bed in the Family/Community Gua for family members.

If your usual visitors are relatives, place the guest room bed(s) in the Family/Community Gua to emphasize their status as honored family members.

Put the bed in the Helpful People/Travel Gua for friends or colleagues.

If your usual visitors are friends or colleagues, place the guest-room bed(s) in the Helpful People/Travel Gua to define the role they play in your life.

Create a meditation area in a guest room.

A guest room can serve as a quiet, private retreat when it's not being used by guests. In the Wisdom/Knowledge Gua, create a peaceful zone for meditation, contemplation, or prayer. Put a comfortable chair or floor cushion there. Display icons or images that symbolize your beliefs. Burn candles or incense to focus your mind. Play soothing music. Blue, green, and purple are good colors to use to enhance relaxation and spiritual depth.

Chapter 11

Cleaning and Cleansing: Bathrooms

Keep toilet lids down.

Guys, here's an incentive to remember to put that toilet seat down. Chi seeps away from your home via the drains. To prevent the loss of chi, keep toilet lids closed.

Set a live plant on the toilet tank.

Placing a live plant on the tank counteracts the draining effect of the toilet. Chi is drawn to the plant's positive energy instead of slipping away down the drain.

Place a vase of fresh flowers near the bathroom sink.

Like the two previous cures, this one also helps keep chi from draining away. Fresh flowers add a pretty accent in your bathroom, too. Red or orange flowers are best—the fiery yang colors offset the preponderance of yin energy in a bathroom.

Hide the toilet.

Feng shui recommends placing the toilet in the most inconspicuous place—it should not be visible when the bathroom door is open. If this isn't possible in your bathroom, consider placing a screen, curtain, or other "blind" to hide the toilet.

Use red or orange in your bathroom's color scheme.

To offset the strong yin energy and water element that naturally predominate in a bathroom, choose vibrant fire colors—red or orange—to bring in the yang vibration and create balance. Towels, shower curtains, bath mats, and other accessories will do the trick. If you aren't comfortable with such bright colors, choose a softer tone, such as rose, peach, or even sunny yellow.

Hang a plant in the corner above your bathtub.

This cure, lifts chi and prevents it from flowing down the drain. The mist from your shower or bath nourishes the plant and keeps it healthy, too.

Close the shower curtain.

Closing your shower curtain also helps stop chi from disappearing down the drain.

Use large, bold patterns in your bathroom.

Large designs—especially those that feature triangles or straight lines—activate yang energy. Use bold patterns on towels, shower curtains, or, wallpaper to balance a bathroom's predominant yin energy.

Mist your bathroom with "fire" scents.

Here's another way to correct an imbalance of yin energy and too much of the water element: Mist your bathroom with fiery scents. Warm or spicy fragrances such as clove, cinnamon, amber, sandalwood, and cedar are good choices.

Tie a green ribbon around your showerhead to promote good health.

This cure helps you focus on your health and well-being whenever you shower. Imagine the falling water—which is a source of chi—washing away any impurities, illnesses, or other health problems. The green ribbon represents life, growth, and serenity.

Use odd numbers in your bathroom.

Odd numbers are considered yang. By using an odd number of objects—three towels instead of two, for instance—in your bathroom, you help counteract the predominance of yin energy that's usually present.

Tie a gold ribbon around your showerhead to attract prosperity.

This simple cure reminds you to focus on prosperity while you shower. The gold ribbon symbolizes wealth, and falling water is a source of chi. Together, they represent blessings and abundance flowing down on you.

Burn candles while bathing.

Taking a bath by candlelight is both relaxing and romantic. From the perspective of feng shui, burning candles in your bathroom provides another benefit, too: Candles help offset a predominance of yin energy by adding the fire element, which is often missing or underrepresented in bathrooms.

Hang a mirror on the outside of the bathroom door.

Here, the mirror serves to deflect chi away from the bathroom and prevents it from slipping away down the drains.

Close the bathroom door.

If you have a bathroom that opens into the kitchen, keep the door closed. This prevents the prosperity generated in the kitchen from being sucked away by the bathroom.

Hang pictures in your bathroom that depict good health.

Because the bathroom is connected with health, hang images here that suggest good health and well-being.

Install good lighting above your sink.

From a practical standpoint, good lighting lets you see to shave or put on makeup. Symbolically, a bright light above your sink is a "fire" cure that counteracts the powerful yin energy of water.

Add lavender essential oil to bathwater to enhance relaxation.

Lavender essential oil soothes the mind and nerves and has a calming effect on the entire body, especially when added to bathwater. Take a hot, soothing, lavender-scented bath before bed to wash away the stress of the day and improve your sleep.

Use baskets in your bathroom.

Baskets bring texture and the wood element into your bathroom, offsetting a predominance of the water element. They're also great for storing and organizing everything from extra rolls of toilet paper to cosmetics to guest towels.

Place a quartz crystal on your bathroom windowsill.

Crystals attract light and augment the fire element. Bathrooms tend to contain too much yin energy; this cure is an easy way to add a little yang to the mix.

Perform a cleansing ritual to improve health.

The bathroom is linked with health because we cleanse and purify ourselves here. Rather than thinking only of the cleansing aspect, turn your daily washing routine into a healing ritual. Baths, for instance, have long been enjoyed for their healing and calming benefits—especially when combined with aromatherapy bath salts or oils. Wash away stress and cares along with dirt to boost your health and well-being on every level.

Use aromatherapy soap.

Many companies now scent soap with essential oils to produce aromatherapy effects. Clean-smelling mint and citrus fragrances stimulate the senses and encourage mental clarity—they're good to use first thing in the morning. Floral scents such as rose, lilac, lily of the valley, jasmine, and ylang-ylang promote affectionate feelings and congeniality. Spicy aromas—cinnamon, clove, carnation, ginger, and amber—are energizing and invigorating.

Add texture to your bathroom.

Smooth surfaces—tile, porcelain, glass, stainless steel—predominate in most bathrooms. To create balance, add richly textured materials wherever possible; try plush towels and bath mats, a cloth shower curtain instead of glass doors, thick curtains, or textured wallpaper. Accessories made from rough, nubby, or nappy materials are good choices, too, instead of the usual smooth plastic or ceramic items.

Hang an attractive piece of artwork above the toilet.

Another way to keep chi from being flushed away is to hang an attractive picture above the toilet. This redirects chi's focus upward, rather than down the drain.

Install a ceiling fan in your bathroom.

Like many feng shui cures, this one has both a practical and a symbolic side. A ceiling fan helps draw dampness out of the bathroom to prevent mold and mildew. A fan also circulates chi and keeps it from seeping away down the drains.

Repair leaky faucets.

Something that's broken or malfunctioning in the bathroom can be a sign of health woes. And, because water is linked with prosperity in feng shui, a leaky faucet may signify that your money is going down the drain. Fix it before it leads to problems in either area.

Fix a toilet that "runs."

This situation is similar to the previous one. A toilet that continually runs can suggest that your money is leaking away. It may also lead to diminished vitality or indicate that your energy is being drained off. Repair it to prevent money or health problems.

Clean out your medicine cabinet regularly.

Medications whose shelf lives have lapsed can be less effective than new ones. Periodically, go through your medicine cabinet and throw out old prescriptions and over-the-counter medications.

Eliminate clutter in your bathroom.

Because the bathroom is linked with health, your physical well-being may be hampered if you allow clutter to collect in this room. Keep your bathroom clean and clear to promote good health.

Include wood in your bathroom décor.

The wood element is missing in many bathrooms. If your bath doesn't feature a wooden vanity cabinet, add accessories made of wood, such as a wooden toilet seat, pegboard, or towel bar, or a mirror or pictures with wooden frames, to create balance.

Bathrooms describe whoever uses them most often.

If you have more than one bathroom in your home, consider who uses each most often. A bathroom connected to the master bedroom, for instance, will influence the health and well-being of the principal adult(s) in the household. A bathroom that's used mainly by the children in the family describes them. Guest baths are linked with visitors. Examine the bathrooms in your home according to this guideline; then use feng shui cures as needed.

Chapter 12

Financial Planning: The Home Office

Position your desk so you can see the door.

Arrange your office furniture so that when you are seated at your desk you can easily see the entrance door. If your back is to the door, you may not be able to concentrate—you'll always be on guard because, subconsciously, you know that someone could enter your office without your knowledge.

Place a mirror so you can see the door to your office.

If you can't position your desk so that you can see the entrance to your office while seated, hang a mirror on the wall so that it reflects the doorway. This cure lets you glance in the mirror without having to turn around and helps avoid distractions.

Clean out your file cabinets regularly.

If you let "old business" fill up your file cabinets, you may prevent new business from coming your way. Go through your files and update them regularly. Remove paperwork that's no longer current. A good rule of thumb is to leave about one-third of your file cabinets empty to indicate that you are ready to receive new business.

Use wooden furniture to encourage expansion.

In the Chinese elemental system, wood is linked with growth. To help your business or finances increase, furnish your office with wooden furniture.

Keep your desktop free of clutter.

Your desktop should be considered "prime real estate," and only items you use daily should be allocated space on this work surface. A cluttered desktop is not only inefficient and unattractive, but it can also signify that you are too busy to handle your current business, let alone take on anything new. Clutter is also a symbol of confusion and lack of focus. By cleaning and organizing your desk, you demonstrate a willingness to get your financial and business life in order.

Use the bagua to analyze your desk.

You can superimpose the bagua on your desktop to see which sections of your desk correspond to which areas of your work life. Position the octagon so that the Self/Identity Gua aligns with the desk's kneehole space and the Fame/Future Gua points toward the back of your desk. Now, arrange your files, computer, communication equipment, and office supplies in the appropriate sectors. (Refer to Chapter 2, Looking Inside, on page 29 for more information.)

Update your Rolodex regularly.

Cull old names and addresses from your Rolodex on a regular basis. You won't waste time looking through the cards of people you'll never contact again, and you'll symbolically make room for new people to enter your life.

TIP: Place your Rolodex in the Helpful People/Travel Gua of your office or on the section of your desktop that corresponds to this gua.

Place your phone in the Helpful People/Travel Gua.

This symbolic cure can facilitate communication with customers, suppliers, coworkers, and colleagues. In feng shui, "helpful people" also refers to the people who assist you in your business and personal affairs—doctors, accountants, lawyers, agents, and so on. The more you communicate with associates, the more benefits you'll receive from placing your phone in this gua.

Fix or replace damaged office equipment.

Broken or damaged equipment in your office symbolizes broken deals or promises, damaged relationships with customers or suppliers, and other problems. Repair or replace any office machines, computers, or furnishings promptly to keep your business running smoothly.

Use metal furnishings to promote stability.

The metal element in feng shui increases strength and permanence. If your goal is to improve stability or structure in your company's business or finances, choose metal furnishings for your office.

Reduce employee turnover with metal desks.

Does your company have a problem with employee turnover? Choose metal desks for your staff—the metal element increases stability. This cure can also encourage irresponsible employees to be more reliable and determined.

Display artwork in your Creativity/Children Gua.

To inspire your own creativity, place pictures or sculpture by an artist you admire in the Creativity/Children Gua of your office. Or display your own creations here.

Put an aquarium in your Fame/Future or Wealth Gua.

In China, fish are considered symbols of good fortune, career success, and prosperity—particularly goldfish (or koi). To attract these blessings, place an aquarium in the Fame/Future Gua or the Wealth Gua of your office.

Use an image of fish to attract prosperity.

If you don't want to install an aquarium, you can still use the lucky symbolism associated with fish to attract wealth and success. Hang a painting or display another image of fish in the Fame/Future or Wealth Gua of your office.

Use peach in your Family/Community Gua.

Peach combines the optimism of yellow with the good luck of red. To enhance relationships with those in your near vicinity, place something peach or coral-colored in the Family/Community Gua of your office. This cure is especially good for people whose business activities are centered in their neighborhoods or communities, or who are involved in family enterprises.

Use a black phone to encourage prosperous communication with colleagues and customers.

Black is considered a fortunate color in China because it is associated with wealth. It's also a "water" color, which emphasizes qualities such as flexibility and cooperation. Using a black phone can help stimulate business and prosperity—especially if your work involves a lot of telephone contact. Salespeople in particular can benefit from this cure.

Use black in your decorating scheme to increase prosperity.

Incorporating black, the Chinese color of wealth, into your office color scheme can help improve your prosperity. A black leather desk chair or black file cabinets are obvious choices, but a sleek black desk could be an attractive item, too.

Put something black in the Wealth Gua of your office.

If you find black furniture too heavy or dark, at least place something black in your office's Wealth Gua, such as a black china vase full of fresh flowers.

Use white in your decorating scheme to promote stability and structure.

White is linked with the metal element in feng shui, so including this color in your office can help provide structure. If your goal is to increase stability and order in your business or finances, incorporate white into your color scheme.

Choose a gray carpet to improve security.

Gray is also a "metal" color and can enhance stability in your business. By placing a gray carpet underfoot, you symbolically establish a sound foundation in your workplace and improve your own (or your employees') sense of security.

Use yellow in your decorating scheme to encourage optimism and creative thinking.

Sunny yellow helps us feel more cheerful and positive. To boost your spirits and stimulate creative thinking, paint your office walls yellow.

Paint your office door red.

Share good luck with everyone who enters your office by painting the door red, the Chinese color of luck. Each time you go in or out, you'll remind your subconscious to bring good luck your way.

Tie a red ribbon around your office doorknob.

If you choose not to paint your door red, at least tie a red ribbon around your doorknob. This less dramatic cure can also help attract good luck to you and your business.

Paint your office door green to increase prosperity.

Because green is the color of money in some countries, you can attract financial growth to your business by painting your office door green. In feng shui, green is considered an "earth" color and, as such, it encourages security, comfort, and stability in financial areas.

Place your computer in the Wealth Gua of your office.

If you're like many people, the computer is an essential part of your business. Electronic equipment also helps activate matters associated with the gua where it's placed. Therefore, if you want to stimulate prosperity, position the computer in your Wealth Gua.

Display your logo in the Self/Identity Gua.

A logo is an important symbol that represents you and the work you do. If you have a logo, display it prominently in the Self/Identity Gua of your office.

Place promotional materials in the Self/Identity Gua of your office.

The Self/Identity Gua is also a good place to put business cards, pamphlets, catalogs, advertising literature, and other promotional materials. Anything that you connect with your own or your company's professional image belongs in this sector of your office.

Display an image of your ideal self in the Self/Identity Gua.

To reinforce your sense of self and your professional image, display a picture, icon, or other symbol of your ideal in the Self/Identity Gua of your office. For example, a screenwriter I know has a picture of an Oscar hanging in her Self/Identity Gua.

Rearrange your office furniture periodically.

To encourage new business and stimulate new opportunities in your work life, rearrange the furniture in your office periodically. Once a year may be often enough, unless you find yourself getting into a rut. By changing your interior, you'll change things in the outer world, too.

Keep the passageways in your office free of obstacles and clutter.

Chi moves through your office in much the same way you do. If your office's passageways are blocked with obstacles or clutter, chi can't flow smoothly to nurture your business and finances. Clutter also suggests confusion, old ideas or behaviors, and problems. To keep your business moving forward in an unhampered manner, clear clutter and other obstructions from your office walkways. (See my books *10-Minute Clutter Control* and *10-Minute Clutter Control Room by Room* for more information.)

Put the number one in your Self/Identity Gua.

You're number one—make it clear by displaying this number in your Self/Identity Gua.

Use dragons to enhance your reputation.

The Chinese consider dragons to be symbols of success and good luck. Display an image of a dragon in the Fame/Future Gua of your office to enhance your reputation or public image.

Hang a wind chime in your Wealth Gua.

To stir up new business or prevent your finances from stagnating, place a wind chime in the Wealth Gua of your office. This cure combines movement with sound to stimulate prosperity. (Note: If there's no wind in your office to make the chimes ring, touch them periodically so they work their magic.)

Clean off your desk at the end of each day.

Before you close up shop for the night, clear your desktop. The next time you come into your office, you won't feel intimidated by seeing piles of work waiting for you.

Tie a red ribbon around paid bills.

After you pay your bills, place them in a box and tie a red ribbon around them. This action shows you are confident that you will always have enough money to pay your bills on time.

Keep closet doors shut.

Because closets represent private matters, it's usually best to keep their doors closed so your "secrets" don't leak out into your business environment.

Put live plants in your office.

As one of the most popular feng shui cures, plants symbolize growth and life. Their green foliage also represents the color of money in some countries. Place one or more healthy plants in your office to encourage the growth and prosperity of your business.

TIP: Keep plants neatly trimmed. Dead leaves and scraggly vines signify conditions that you don't want to be part of your work life.

Replace low-wattage lightbulbs with brighter ones.

Another commonly used feng shui cure, this one augments the "fire" element in your office. In both Eastern and Western cosmologies, fire is stimulating, energizing, and exciting. Chi is drawn to light, too, so you can increase the amount of chi in your office simply by replacing low-wattage lightbulbs with brighter ones.

Wash the windows in your office.

In feng shui, windows symbolize the eyes. To see business or financial situations more clearly, wash the windows in your office.

Use a leather desk chair to improve cooperation.

Leather and other smooth fabrics come under the “water” element, whose qualities include adaptability and blending. To improve cooperation with your coworkers, employees, colleagues, or customers, choose a leather desk chair (black is best). If you have employees who don’t get along or who tend to be too rigid, consider giving them leather chairs to increase their flexibility.

Arrange books and reference materials in your Wisdom/Knowledge Gua.

The logical place for books and reference texts is in your office’s Wisdom/Knowledge Gua. Place educational materials in this sector of your office to encourage intellectual growth.

Use a paperweight made of onyx or obsidian.

These black stones are considered fortunate for attracting money. Heavy objects serve to hold things down, literally and symbolically, so paperweights made of onyx or obsidian can prevent money from flowing out too quickly. People who work with the energies of stones also find that the vibrations in onyx and obsidian enhance practicality and determination, which are desirable qualities in the business world.

Remove pointed objects from your Helpful People/Travel Gua.

Pointed objects, such as scissors and letter openers, can cause problems with coworkers, customers, or colleagues, especially in the area of communication. The points and edges symbolize cutting words or sharp remarks. Move sharp items out of the Helpful People/Travel Gua to avoid arguments with business associates.

Put three coins in a red envelope and place it in your Wealth Gua. In feng shui, money is often placed in a red envelope to attract luck and demonstrate trust. It's common practice to use a red envelope to pay a feng shui practitioner. To boost your financial abundance, put three coins in a red envelope and place it in your Wealth Gua. Three is an auspicious number because it is linked with change and creativity, so the three coins can help stir up new business opportunities. Three coins are sometimes used to consult the ancient Chinese book of wisdom, the *I Ching*; therefore, this cure can also show your desire to receive insight and guidance in business or financial matters from a higher source.

TIP: Red is a stimulating color, which always makes it a good choice for rooms where activity takes place, such as your home office.

Burn citrus-scented incense in your office.

The study of aromatherapy has shown that scents influence us on a deep emotional and psychological level. The clean, fresh aroma of citrus (orange, lemon, or lime) stimulates and clears the mind. If you feel tired or confused, burn citrus-scented incense in your office to "wake up" your senses and jump-start your thinking process.

Burn peppermint incense in your office.

In some Western schools of thought, peppermint is linked with prosperity. In the East, incense is used to send messages and requests to the higher realms. Burn peppermint-scented incense in your office daily to attract financial gains and opportunities.

Hang a picture that symbolizes success in your Fame/Future Gua.
What says "success" to you? A Rolls Royce? A castle? A trophy? Frame a picture of something that depicts your image of success and hang it in the Fame/Future Gua of your office. Every time you look at it, you'll remind yourself of your intention and reinforce your goal to achieve success.

Store atlases, maps, and travel books in the Helpful People/Travel Gua.
If you'd like to expand your business into other areas or want to travel more, place atlases, maps, a globe, or other travel-related materials in the Helpful People/Travel Gua of your office.

Place diplomas, awards, or certifications in your Fame/Future Gua.
These symbols of your success can fuel future accomplishments if you hang them in your office's Fame/Future Gua. Each time you look at them, you'll be reminded of your capabilities and be spurred to keep reaching for greater rewards.

Frame a hundred-dollar bill and display it in your Wealth Gua.

This cure has an obvious and powerful impact on your subconscious. Display a hundred-dollar bill in your Wealth Gua to attract money. Use a wooden frame if financial growth is your objective, and a metal one if you want to secure your money and limit expenditures.

Avoid placing your desk under a slanted ceiling or heavy beam.

Slanted ceilings and heavy exposed beams can depress chi and limit the amount of positive energy available for your business endeavors. Don't position your desk beneath eaves or beams—you may have to work harder to achieve the success you desire.

Hang an octagon-shaped mirror in your Wealth Gua.

In the study of numerology, eight is the number of financial success and business. (It's no accident that 800 became the toll-free telephone number of businesses.) In China, the octagon—the bagua's shape—is considered fortunate, so hang an eight-sided mirror in your office's Wealth Gua to attract abundance of all kinds.

Place a safe or cash box in the Wealth Gua.

If you keep a safe or cash box in your office, put it in the Wealth Gua to encourage prosperity.

Balance angles and straight lines with curves and waves.

Offices generally include lots of straight lines and angles—desks, bookcases, file cabinets, and computer equipment are all rectangular or square. You can reduce the stress caused by a preponderance of straight lines by introducing curves and wavy lines into your office. Choose fabrics, carpeting, or wallpaper with flowing, rounded shapes to create balance. My office, for instance, has a floral dhurrie rug, wallpaper patterned with vines, and a round clock.

Incorporate the earth element into in your office to increase security, comfort, and calm.

Many office environments contain elemental imbalances—they may feature lots of metal or wood but be weak in the earth element. To counteract this and make your office more comfortable and peaceful, add circles, ceramic or stone accessories, earth colors (brown, yellow), or thick area rugs.

About the Author

Skye Alexander is the author of numerous mind-body-spirit books, including *10-Minute Feng Shui, 10-Minute Clutter Control, 10-Minute Clutter Control Room by Room, 10-Minute Magic Spells, 10-Minute Tarot, 10-Minute Crystal Ball, The Care and Feeding of Your Chi, Magickal Astrology,* and *Planets in Signs.* She also writes fiction, and her first mystery novel, *Hidden Agenda,* won the Kiss of Death Award for the year's best book of romantic suspense. Her stories have appeared in several anthologies, including *Undertow, Riptide, Windchill,* and *Fenway Fiction,* and they have been translated into German, Portuguese, and Korean. In 2001, she was filmed for a Discovery Channel special performing a magic ritual at Stonehenge. After living in Massachusetts for thirty years, she and her feline assistant, Domino, will soon reside in Texas.

Other books in the "10-Minute" series available from Fair Winds Press

10-Minute Clutter Control
By Skye Alexander
ISBN: 1-59233-068-1
$12.00

10-Minute Feng Shui
By Skye Alexander
ISBN: 1-931421-88-X
$12.00

10-Minute Housekeeping
By Rose R. Kennedy
ISBN: 1-59233-177-7
$12.00

10-Minute Organizing
By Sara Lavieri Hunter
ISBN: 1-59233-181-5
$12.00

10-Minute Home Repairs
By Jerri Farris
ISBN: 1-59233-203-X
$12.00

10-Minute Energy-Saving Secrets
By Jerri Farris
ISBN: 1-59233-245-5
$12.00